I0459203

Free Your

MIND

Are you tired of feeling trapped by overthinking, negative thoughts, and mental clutter? Free Your MIND is a practical and inspiring guide to breaking free from the invisible chains that hold you back.

Written by

ERIC LEBOUTHILLIER

AcraPublishing | 2025 1st Edition

Preface

This book was born from a simple truth: our greatest battles are often fought in the mind. Every day, countless thoughts run through us — some lift us higher, others weigh us down. I wrote Free Your MIND to give you the tools, clarity, and confidence to break free from what holds you back and step into a life of focus, peace, and purpose.

You don't need complicated systems or years of training to change your life. You need practical steps, easy-to-follow guidance, and the courage to begin. This book is your invitation to do just that.

Who this book is for

Free Your MIND is written for anyone who feels trapped by constant mental noise, negative thoughts, or the weight of overthinking. If you've ever wished you could silence the chaos inside your head and finally find clarity, this book is for you. It's designed to guide ordinary people — from busy professionals to students, parents, and anyone in between — toward a calmer, sharper, and freer state of mind.

You'll find this book especially valuable if you:

- Struggle with **overthinking** or replaying the same thoughts over and over.
- Battle **negative self-talk** and limiting beliefs that hold you back.
- Feel easily **distracted** or mentally exhausted from constant stimulation.
- Long for **mental clarity, calm, and emotional balance** in your daily life.
- Want practical strategies for creating lasting inner peace and focus.

What to expect from this book

This book is not theory-heavy or complicated — it's a practical guide packed with powerful insights and simple tools you can start using right away. Each chapter is crafted to help you clear mental clutter, reprogram limiting patterns, and build a healthier, freer mindset step by step.

Inside, you'll discover:

- **10 transformative chapters** that break down mental traps and show you how to escape them.
- **Science-backed insights** into how your brain works and why it sometimes sabotages you.
- **Daily practices and exercises** to quiet your thoughts and sharpen your focus.
- **Proven methods** to reduce stress, stop overthinking, and strengthen resilience.
- A **practical roadmap** to create lasting clarity, peace, and inner freedom.

Any trademarks, service marks, product names, or named features referenced in this book are the property of their respective owners. The author and publisher make no claim of ownership and do not endorse any third-party products or services by including them in this publication.

LEGAL DISCLAIMER

This publication is intended solely for informational and educational purposes. It does not constitute legal, financial, medical, or professional advice. The content is not a substitute for consultation with qualified experts or licensed professionals in the relevant fields.

Portions of this work have been created or assisted by artificial intelligence (AI) tools. While every reasonable effort has been made to review, fact-check, and edit the content for clarity and accuracy, AI-generated information may occasionally contain errors, omissions, or generalized statements. The author and publisher do not guarantee the accuracy, completeness, or reliability of the information provided.

Readers are strongly encouraged to seek independent advice tailored to their personal circumstances from qualified legal, financial, healthcare, or compliance professionals before making decisions or taking action based on this content.

References to specific products, services, companies, websites, or technologies do not imply endorsement or affiliation unless explicitly stated. All trademarks and brand names mentioned remain the property of their respective owners.

The author and publisher disclaim any liability, loss, or risk incurred directly or indirectly from the use or misuse of this publication. This includes, but is not limited to, damages of any kind — including incidental, special, or consequential — arising out of the reliance on the material presented.

All references to laws, regulations, security standards, or industry guidelines are intended for general awareness only and may not reflect the most current legal developments. This publication is not intended to create, and receipt does not constitute, a client relationship with the author, publisher, or any affiliated entity.

By reading, accessing, or applying the content in this publication, you agree to do so at your own risk. If you do not accept these terms, you are advised to discontinue use of this material immediately.

Table of Contents

CHAPTER 1

Understanding Mental Traps

The Invisible Chains: How Limiting Beliefs Form

Every human being walks through life with a set of invisible scripts running in the background of their mind. These scripts are not consciously chosen; they are absorbed, reinforced, and repeated until they feel like unquestionable truths. They whisper rules about what is possible, what is not, and what is "realistic." These scripts are limiting beliefs, and they operate like invisible chains. You may not see them, but they dictate where you go, how you behave, and what you allow yourself to pursue. To understand mental freedom, we must first uncover how these chains are formed.

Limiting beliefs are not created overnight. They are constructed through countless experiences, small remarks, cultural norms, and personal interpretations. Over time, they crystallize into mental patterns that filter how we perceive ourselves and the world. They determine whether we take a leap or hold back, whether we voice an opinion or stay silent, whether we step into growth or remain in the comfort zone.

Understanding how limiting beliefs form is the first step toward dismantling them. By tracing their origins, we begin to recognize that they are not absolute truths, but rather learned interpretations. And if they were learned, they can also be unlearned.

Early Imprints: The Childhood Blueprint

Most limiting beliefs begin in childhood, when our minds are impressionable and we rely heavily on external authority figures for guidance. During the early years, children absorb messages from parents, teachers, and peers with little filter. The brain at this stage is highly plastic, designed to learn rapidly. Unfortunately, this openness means both empowering and disempowering messages take root deeply.

For example, a child who hears "You're so clumsy" after dropping a glass may internalize not just the act of being clumsy, but an identity around it. Soon, they may avoid activities that require physical coordination, convinced that they are "not the type" who can succeed in them. Another child may be told "Math isn't really for you" after struggling with arithmetic. That comment, though casual, might grow into a lifelong belief that they are incapable of analytical thinking.

Research in developmental psychology shows that children form "core beliefs" between the ages of three and ten. These are the mental building blocks of self-concept. A repeated message during this phase—whether spoken or implied—can become a foundational assumption about who they are and what they can achieve. Importantly, these beliefs are not formed only by what is said explicitly. Silence can be just as powerful. When a child's efforts go unacknowledged, they may believe they are unworthy of attention. When their emotions are dismissed, they may believe their feelings are not valid.

The power of early imprints explains why two people from similar environments may develop vastly different mindsets. The subtle cues they picked up, the way events were interpreted, and the emotional responses they received created unique mental filters. These filters evolve into the invisible chains that shape adulthood.

Cultural Narratives: The Weight of Collective Beliefs

Beyond family, culture plays a profound role in shaping limiting beliefs. Every society carries collective narratives—ideas about success, failure, gender roles, intelligence, beauty, or morality. These narratives are often presented as objective truths, but they are deeply influenced by tradition and history.

For instance, in some cultures, conformity is valued above individuality. A child who expresses a strong personal interest may be told to "fit in" or avoid drawing attention. The resulting belief might be: "It is dangerous to stand out." In other cultures, achievement is measured almost exclusively by financial success. Someone growing up in this context may internalize the idea: "If I am not wealthy, I am not valuable."

Cultural narratives also affect how we interpret setbacks. In societies where failure is stigmatized, mistakes are often equated with incompetence. Children in such environments may form the belief that failure is unbearable, leading them to avoid risks altogether. Conversely, cultures that normalize trial and error often raise individuals with more resilient and growth-oriented mindsets.

The critical point is that cultural beliefs, while shared by many, are not universal truths. They are inherited assumptions. Without questioning them, individuals carry the weight of these narratives, mistaking them for personal limitations rather than cultural conditioning.

The Role of Repetition and Confirmation Bias

A single comment or event may plant the seed of a limiting belief, but repetition allows it to grow into a dominant narrative. Each time a belief is reinforced—through similar experiences, repeated messages, or internal dialogue—it gains strength.

Take the example of someone who believes they are "not creative." This belief might begin with a childhood art project that received poor feedback. Over time, each instance of struggling with a creative task reinforces the belief. Eventually, they stop attempting creative endeavors altogether, which eliminates opportunities to disprove the belief. This is confirmation bias in action: the tendency to notice and remember evidence that supports what we already believe while ignoring or discounting evidence that contradicts it.

Once a belief is in place, the brain actively filters reality to preserve it. If a person believes they are bad at public speaking, they will notice every stumble and forget every compliment. If they believe they are unlucky in relationships, they will remember rejections vividly while minimizing moments of connection. This mental filter ensures that the limiting belief feels increasingly "true," even though it is only a selective perception of reality.

Repetition solidifies beliefs not only through external feedback but also through self-talk. Each time we tell ourselves, "I can't do this," "I'm not good enough," or "This never works out for me," we are deepening the neural pathway of that belief. Over months and years, these repeated thoughts become automatic, shaping how we respond to challenges before we even realize it.

Trauma and Emotional Encoding

Not all limiting beliefs arise gradually. Some are forged in moments of intense emotional pain. Trauma—whether acute, like a car accident, or relational, like ongoing neglect—can create powerful mental associations that linger long after the event.

Consider a child who speaks up in class and is laughed at by peers. The embarrassment may imprint a belief that "speaking up is dangerous." Another example: someone who experiences betrayal in a close relationship may adopt the belief that "no one can be trusted." While these beliefs may have been protective in the immediate aftermath—helping the person avoid further harm—they become limiting when applied universally.

Neuroscience explains why emotional experiences shape beliefs so powerfully. The amygdala, the brain's fear center, tags emotionally intense moments as highly significant. The brain then encodes these experiences more vividly, making the associated beliefs harder to dislodge. That is why even a single traumatic event can alter self-perception for decades.

Understanding this mechanism is critical. It helps us see that limiting beliefs formed in trauma are not evidence of weakness or irrationality; they are the mind's way of protecting us. The challenge is learning to recognize when a protective belief has outlived its usefulness and is now keeping us trapped.

Social Comparison and the Myth of "Enough"

Another powerful source of limiting beliefs is comparison. From early schooling to social media, humans are constantly measuring themselves against others. While comparison can sometimes inspire growth, it often reinforces a sense of inadequacy.

In the classroom, a child who consistently scores below average may adopt the belief: "I am not intelligent." On social media, where people display curated versions of their lives, someone may conclude: "I am not attractive enough," or "I am not successful enough." These beliefs are insidious because the standard of comparison is often unrealistic or selective.

Psychologists describe this as the "myth of enough"—the idea that whatever we are, it is never sufficient compared to someone else. This belief drives perfectionism, chronic dissatisfaction, and fear of failure. It narrows the field of what feels achievable, because the individual is perpetually chasing an elusive standard.

Breaking free from the myth of "enough" requires recognizing that comparison is a mental trap, not a reflection of absolute truth. Others' achievements or appearances do not diminish one's own potential, yet the mind often interprets them that way. This distorted interpretation feeds limiting beliefs about capability, worth, and possibility.

The Authority Effect: When Experts Shape Our Limits

Limiting beliefs are often cemented by authority figures—teachers, coaches, bosses, or even doctors—whose words carry added weight. Because these figures are seen as knowledgeable, their judgments are internalized as fact, even when they are inaccurate.

For instance, a student who hears from a teacher that they "will never be good at science" may accept this as an unquestionable truth. A young athlete criticized by a coach may decide they "don't have what it takes" to succeed. Even well-meaning authority figures can unintentionally impose limits. A doctor telling a patient that recovery is unlikely might reinforce a belief that healing is impossible, even when alternative perspectives suggest otherwise.

The authority effect is amplified because humans are wired to respect hierarchy. Studies in social psychology show that people are more likely to believe and obey instructions from perceived experts, even against their own judgment. While this tendency has evolutionary advantages—it allows societies to function smoothly—it also means that harmful comments from authority figures can shape a person's belief system disproportionately.

Recognizing the authority effect helps us question whether our limits are truly ours or simply borrowed from someone else's opinion.

How Limiting Beliefs Hide in Plain Sight

One of the most challenging aspects of limiting beliefs is that they often go unnoticed. Unlike obvious fears or phobias, limiting beliefs feel like neutral observations. A person might say, "I'm just not good with money" or "I've never been creative," as if they were describing the color of their hair. Because these beliefs masquerade as facts, they are rarely scrutinized.

This invisibility is what makes them so powerful. They silently influence decisions, often without conscious awareness. Someone who believes "I don't deserve happiness" may sabotage relationships without realizing why. Someone who believes "I am not a leader" may avoid opportunities for growth, assuming they are not meant for them.

Bringing these beliefs into awareness requires deliberate reflection. Questions like "Where did this belief come from?" or "Whose voice am I repeating?" can expose the hidden assumptions behind self-limiting statements. Once recognized, beliefs lose part of their power, because they are revealed as interpretations rather than truths.

Transforming Awareness into Freedom

Understanding how limiting beliefs form is not merely an intellectual exercise; it is the foundation for change. Once we see that beliefs are constructed—from childhood imprints, cultural narratives, repetition, trauma, comparison, or authority—we realize they are not permanent. They are mental models, not immutable laws.

Freedom begins when we interrupt the automatic cycle of reinforcement. Instead of accepting every self-critical thought as fact, we can challenge it. Instead of repeating inherited cultural narratives, we can ask whether they align with our values. Instead of letting past trauma dictate present choices, we can acknowledge its influence while consciously rewriting our story.

This process does not happen overnight. Just as beliefs were formed through repetition, they are dismantled through repeated questioning, reframing, and new experiences. But every time we challenge a limiting belief, we weaken its hold. Every time we act in defiance of it, we create evidence for a new, more empowering narrative.

Takeaway: Seeing the Chains to Break Them

Limiting beliefs are the invisible chains that bind the mind, but they are not unbreakable. They are formed through early imprints, cultural conditioning, repetition, trauma, comparison, and the influence of authority. They hide in plain sight, masquerading as facts about who we are and what is possible.

The first step to mental freedom is recognizing that these chains exist. Once we see how they were forged, we can begin the work of dismantling them. Awareness transforms beliefs from unquestioned truths into choices. And in that moment of recognition, a door opens—a door to clarity, focus, and the possibility of living a life defined not by invisible chains, but by conscious freedom.

The Role of Negative Self-Talk in Daily Life

Inside every person's mind is a constant stream of dialogue. Sometimes this inner voice is supportive, offering encouragement, focus, and clarity. At other times, it is critical, harsh, and unforgiving. This latter pattern is what psychologists call negative self-talk—the running commentary that magnifies mistakes, minimizes achievements, and predicts failure before it even happens. While it might seem like a minor annoyance, negative self-talk plays an enormous role in shaping daily life. It influences decisions, emotions, relationships, and even physical health.

To understand mental freedom, we must first understand how this inner dialogue operates, why it feels so convincing, and how it quietly limits our lives.

What Negative Self-Talk Really Is

Negative self-talk is not simply being realistic or cautious. It is the habitual interpretation of events, actions, and possibilities through a lens of self-criticism and doubt. It is the difference between saying, "I made a mistake, but I'll do better next time" and saying, "I'm such an idiot; I always mess things up."

Researchers categorize negative self-talk into four main patterns:

1. **Filtering** – focusing only on the negative aspects of a situation while ignoring the positives.
2. **Catastrophizing** – expecting the worst possible outcome in every scenario.
3. **Personalizing** – assuming responsibility for events outside one's control, often with guilt.

4. **Polarizing** – seeing situations as entirely good or entirely bad, with no middle ground.

These patterns don't just describe how someone talks to themselves; they shape how reality is experienced. A person who constantly filters out positives will genuinely perceive their life as bleak, even when good things happen. The inner dialogue doesn't just comment on life—it creates the lens through which life is lived.

How the Inner Critic Is Formed

Negative self-talk rarely begins in adulthood. Like limiting beliefs, it has roots in early experiences. When children hear criticism from authority figures, they often internalize those voices. Over time, the child's own mind repeats those messages automatically, even without external input.

For example, a parent who frequently says, "Why can't you do anything right?" plants a seed that can become a lifelong internal refrain. Even when the parent is no longer present, the voice echoes internally. Similarly, children who are praised only for achievements, rather than for effort or character, may grow into adults whose inner voices demand perfection and punish every mistake.

The inner critic is also reinforced by cultural conditioning. Societies that value competition often normalize harsh self-comparison. Social media amplifies this effect, as people measure themselves against curated images of others' lives. Over time, the brain learns to mimic this external judgment, creating an internalized critic that never rests.

The Daily Impact of Negative Self-Talk

The influence of negative self-talk is pervasive, affecting nearly every domain of life.

1. Decision-Making

When the inner critic dominates, decisions become paralyzed. For instance, someone may avoid applying for a job because the voice says, "You're not qualified enough." They may hesitate to speak in a meeting because the voice whispers, "Everyone will think you sound stupid." Opportunities pass by, not because the individual lacks ability, but because their inner dialogue convinces them not to try.

2. Emotional Health

Negative self-talk is strongly correlated with anxiety and depression. A mind that constantly predicts failure or criticizes every action produces chronic stress. The body responds with elevated cortisol, which can lead to fatigue, irritability, and difficulty concentrating. Over time, this mental pattern can become a self-fulfilling prophecy: the more someone expects negative outcomes, the more they interpret experiences in a way that confirms those expectations.

3. Relationships

Self-talk does not stay confined within the mind; it spills into interactions with others. Someone who constantly tells themselves, "I am unworthy of love," may sabotage relationships by pushing people away or tolerating mistreatment. Someone who believes, "I'm always a burden," may withhold their needs, leading to unbalanced connections. In this way, the internal critic doesn't just harm the individual—it alters the dynamics of every relationship they enter.

4. Performance

Athletes, artists, and professionals alike are hindered by negative self-talk. Studies in sports psychology show that self-criticism reduces performance under pressure, while self-encouragement improves outcomes. A tennis player who mutters "I can't serve today" is far more likely to miss their next serve. The internal dialogue directly shapes confidence, and confidence is a key predictor of success in performance settings.

The Science Behind the Voice

Neuroscience reveals why negative self-talk feels so persistent. The brain's default mode network (DMN)—the system active when the mind is at rest—is heavily involved in self-referential thinking. When idle, the brain naturally turns inward, analyzing the self. For many people, this inward reflection leans negative, as the brain is wired to detect threats.

This negativity bias, an evolutionary mechanism, helped our ancestors survive by paying more attention to dangers than to neutral or positive stimuli. However, in modern life, this bias means the inner dialogue is skewed toward criticism and worry. Instead of scanning the savannah for predators, the brain scans our performance, appearance, and decisions for flaws.

Importantly, repeated self-talk strengthens neural pathways. The more often a thought is repeated, the more automatic it becomes. Over time, negative self-talk can run on autopilot, requiring little conscious input. This explains why many people don't even notice how often they criticize themselves—it has become background noise.

Real-World Illustrations

Consider the case of Maria, a talented graphic designer who consistently produces high-quality work. Despite her achievements, her inner dialogue says, "I'm not creative enough; I just got lucky with this project." As a result, she avoids applying for leadership positions, convinced she will fail. Her colleagues see her as capable, but her internal critic keeps her confined to a smaller role than she deserves.

Or take David, a university student preparing for exams. Each time he sits down to study, his inner voice says, "You're going to fail; you never understand this material." The anxiety from this self-talk makes concentration harder, leading to poor performance, which then confirms his belief. David is trapped in a cycle where self-talk creates the very outcome it predicts.

These examples illustrate a crucial point: negative self-talk is not simply commentary. It actively shapes choices, performance, and self-image. Left unchecked, it becomes a silent architect of limitation.

Breaking the Cycle: Awareness First

The first step in addressing negative self-talk is awareness. Because the inner critic often operates automatically, many people are not even conscious of how harshly they speak to themselves. Journaling is a powerful tool for bringing these patterns into the open. By writing down thoughts, individuals can see on paper what previously felt like background noise. Phrases like "I always fail" or "I'm not good enough" become visible, and visibility is the beginning of change.

Mindfulness practices also help create awareness. By observing thoughts without judgment, individuals learn to notice self-critical dialogue as mental events, not truths. This subtle shift—seeing a thought as a thought, rather than as reality—loosens the grip of the inner critic.

Reframing the Voice

Once negative self-talk is recognized, the next step is reframing. This does not mean replacing every critical thought with blind positivity. Instead, it means challenging distorted thinking with balanced perspectives. For example:

- Instead of "I always fail," try: "I didn't succeed this time, but I can learn from it."

- Instead of "I'm terrible at this," try: "I'm still learning, and improvement takes time."
- Instead of "Everyone thinks I'm stupid," try: "I don't know what others think, but I can prepare and do my best."

Reframing does not deny difficulties; it places them in a constructive context. Over time, repeated reframing rewires the brain, building new neural pathways that support confidence and resilience.

Building an Inner Ally

The ultimate goal is to replace the inner critic with an inner ally—a supportive voice that encourages growth rather than stifles it. This does not happen instantly, but small practices help:

- **Self-Compassion Breaks:** When you notice harsh self-talk, pause and ask, "What would I say to a friend in this situation?" Then, direct those words inward.
- **Evidence Lists:** Keep a record of past successes, no matter how small. Reviewing this list counteracts the brain's negativity bias by reminding it of strengths and achievements.
- **Affirmation with Evidence:** Instead of vague affirmations like "I am amazing," use specific, evidence-based ones: "I prepared thoroughly for this presentation, and I am capable of delivering it."

By consciously cultivating supportive self-talk, individuals train the brain to default toward encouragement rather than criticism.

The Ripple Effect of Changing the Voice

When the inner voice shifts, the impact extends far beyond the individual. Relationships improve as people stop sabotaging themselves or projecting insecurity. Professional opportunities expand as confidence grows. Emotional well-being stabilizes as the constant background noise of criticism fades.

In fact, research shows that cultivating positive self-talk not only boosts confidence but also improves immune function, lowers stress, and increases life satisfaction. The inner dialogue is not just mental—it is physiological. Changing it literally changes the body.

Takeaway: Mastering the Voice Within

Negative self-talk may seem like an invisible companion, but it is one of the most influential forces in daily life. It shapes decisions, emotions, relationships, and performance. Born from early experiences, cultural conditioning, and the brain's natural bias toward threat, it persists because it is repeated and rarely questioned.

But it is not permanent. By bringing awareness to the inner critic, reframing its distortions, and consciously building an inner ally, we can reclaim the power of self-talk. When the voice inside becomes supportive rather than destructive, the entire landscape of life changes.

Freedom begins not when the world stops criticizing, but when we stop doing the world's work for it inside our own minds.

Why Past Experiences Shape Present Reactions

Every moment of your present life is filtered through the lens of your past. When you react to a situation—whether with joy, fear, hesitation, or confidence—you are rarely responding only to what is in front of you. Instead, your brain is drawing from a vast archive of experiences, memories, and emotional imprints to decide how to interpret the moment. This is why two people can encounter the same event and respond in completely different ways. One might see a challenge as an exciting opportunity, while another perceives it as a looming threat. The difference lies not in the event itself, but in the past experiences shaping perception.

Understanding how past experiences shape present reactions is essential to mental freedom. It helps us see that our responses are not purely objective or rational; they are conditioned, often unconsciously, by what we have lived before. Only by bringing this conditioning into awareness can we begin to respond with choice rather than reflex.

The Brain as a Prediction Machine

Neuroscientists often describe the brain not as a passive receiver of information, but as a prediction machine. Every moment, the brain anticipates what is about to happen, drawing on past data to make sense of the present. This predictive process is efficient: it allows you to react quickly without re-analyzing every detail of every situation.

For example, when you hear a dog bark, your brain doesn't start from zero. It immediately recalls every prior encounter with dogs—whether friendly or aggressive—and uses that archive to interpret the sound. If you were bitten as a child, your brain predicts danger and your body tenses. If you grew up with a loyal family pet, your brain predicts friendliness and you might smile. The bark is the same, but the past determines the meaning.

This predictive function explains why our reactions often feel automatic. They are not random; they are the brain's best guess, based on what has come before. The problem is that the brain does not always distinguish between past and present. A memory of danger can shape responses long after the actual threat has passed, creating limitations in daily life.

Emotional Imprints and the Amygdala

While the brain processes countless pieces of information, emotionally charged experiences are encoded with particular strength. The amygdala—the part of the brain responsible for detecting threats—plays a central role in this process. When something frightening or painful happens, the amygdala tags the memory with a "high importance" marker, ensuring it is remembered vividly.

This is why many people can recall exactly where they were during a traumatic event, even decades later. The emotional intensity seared the experience into memory. From that point forward, the brain treats similar cues—sights, sounds, smells—as potential signals of danger.

Take the example of someone who nearly drowned as a child. Years later, even standing near a swimming pool may trigger anxiety. The logical brain might know they are safe, but the amygdala has linked water with threat. The emotional imprint overrides rational thought, shaping present reactions based on past experience.

The Role of Conditioning

Psychology offers a framework for understanding how past experiences condition present behavior: classical and operant conditioning.

- **Classical conditioning** occurs when a neutral stimulus becomes associated with an emotional response. For instance, if a child is scolded harshly every time they speak up, they may later feel anxious in any situation involving public speaking, even without immediate criticism.
- **Operant conditioning** involves reinforcement. Behaviors followed by rewards are repeated; those followed by punishment are avoided. A student praised for diligence may grow into an adult who feels energized by hard work. A student mocked for asking questions may grow into an adult who avoids seeking help, even when needed.

Both forms of conditioning illustrate how past interactions shape future responses. The brain does not simply record events; it creates patterns of expectation, which then guide behavior.

Implicit Memories: The Hidden Drivers

Not all memories are explicit—conscious and easily recalled. Many past experiences are stored as implicit memories, meaning they influence behavior without conscious awareness. A person may not remember the exact moment they felt rejected, but the feeling of rejection still colors their present relationships.

For example, someone who grew up in an unpredictable household may develop a hyper-vigilant nervous system, constantly scanning for signs of conflict. As an adult, they might overreact to minor disagreements, not because the situation warrants it, but because their body is primed to expect chaos.

Implicit memories are powerful because they bypass rational analysis. You may not know why you feel anxious in a certain context, but the body remembers. This is why some reactions feel "irrational"—they are logical not to the present, but to the past.

Case Studies: Past in Action

Consider Anna, a young professional who struggles with feedback at work. Even mild suggestions from her manager trigger a flood of self-doubt. On the surface, it looks like she is overreacting. But tracing back, Anna grew up with highly critical parents who rarely acknowledged her achievements. Feedback in the present echoes the criticism of the past, activating the same emotional response.

Or take James, who avoids close relationships. Each time someone expresses care for him, he feels uneasy and pulls away. As a child, James experienced abandonment when a caregiver left abruptly. Though he consciously desires intimacy, his nervous system associates closeness with pain. His present behavior is a shield against the wound of the past.

These examples reveal that present struggles often make perfect sense once we see the experiences that shaped them. What looks like irrational avoidance or overreaction is often the brain's way of trying to protect against old pain.

Why Positive Experiences Matter Too

It is easy to focus on how negative experiences shape reactions, but positive experiences are equally influential. A child who was consistently encouraged to try new things may grow into an adult who embraces challenges with enthusiasm. A teenager who felt safe expressing emotions may become an adult with strong emotional intelligence.

These positive imprints show that not all conditioning is limiting. In fact, many strengths—confidence, resilience, curiosity—are the result of past experiences that built supportive internal frameworks. Recognizing this balance is important: while the past can impose chains, it can also provide tools for freedom.

When the Past Hijacks the Present

One of the challenges of past conditioning is that it often operates outside awareness. Someone may say, "That's just the way I am," when in reality, they are replaying learned patterns. Common signs that the past is hijacking the present include:

- **Overreactions** – Responding with disproportionate intensity to minor events.
- **Avoidance** – Staying away from situations that echo past discomfort, even if they are safe.
- **Repetition** – Finding oneself in the same unhealthy patterns repeatedly, such as choosing similar toxic relationships.
- **Numbness** – Disconnecting from emotions because they once felt overwhelming.

These reactions make sense in light of history, but they limit growth if left unexamined.

Breaking the Cycle: Awareness and Reframing

The good news is that while the past shapes the present, it does not have to dictate the future. Mental freedom comes from recognizing when old patterns are at play and consciously choosing new responses.

Awareness begins with self-inquiry. Questions like:

- "When have I felt this way before?"
- "Does this reaction fit the present, or does it belong to the past?"
- "What story am I repeating here?"

Reframing then allows for new interpretations. Instead of seeing feedback as an attack, it can be reframed as support. Instead of viewing intimacy as a threat, it can be reframed as an opportunity for healing connection. Each reframed response builds new neural pathways, gradually weakening the old ones.

The Role of Therapy and Healing Practices

In some cases, past experiences are so deeply ingrained that professional support is essential. Therapies such as cognitive-behavioral therapy (CBT) help individuals identify and challenge distorted thinking rooted in past events. Trauma-focused therapies like EMDR (Eye Movement Desensitization and Reprocessing) help reprocess painful memories so they lose their emotional intensity.

Healing practices outside therapy—such as mindfulness, journaling, and somatic exercises—also support this process. Mindfulness teaches individuals to observe present sensations without judgment, reducing the automatic pull of the past. Journaling allows for re-examining memories and reshaping their narrative. Somatic work helps release the body's stored tension, addressing implicit memories that talk therapy alone cannot reach.

Choosing the Present Over the Past

The ultimate goal is not to erase the past—it cannot be undone—but to loosen its grip on the present. This means acknowledging that reactions make sense given history, while also recognizing that new choices are possible. A person can honor the child who learned to protect themselves with silence while choosing, as an adult, to speak boldly. They can validate the fear that once kept them safe while stepping into courage today.

Takeaway: Freedom Through Awareness

The past is powerful, but it is not destiny. Experiences shape how we react, but they do not define who we must be. By understanding how memories—both explicit and implicit—color perception, we gain the ability to question automatic responses. With awareness, reframing, and healing practices, we can shift from living as echoes of the past to living as conscious creators of the present.

Mental freedom is not about forgetting where we have been. It is about seeing the influence clearly, honoring it, and then choosing the path forward with clarity and intention.

Common Myths About "Mental Freedom"

The idea of mental freedom carries an almost mythical allure. People imagine it as a state of perfect calm, unshakable confidence, or permanent positivity. This fantasy is reinforced by self-help clichés, social media advice, and oversimplified motivational slogans. But the truth is, these misconceptions often make mental freedom harder to achieve. By chasing illusions of what freedom should look like, many overlook what it actually requires.

To move toward genuine clarity and resilience, it is essential to strip away these myths. Mental freedom is not about perfection or escape—it is about awareness, choice, and alignment. Let us explore the most common misconceptions and how they distort the path to real freedom.

Myth 1: Mental Freedom Means Never Having Negative Thoughts

One of the biggest myths is that achieving mental freedom means silencing the mind completely, erasing all negativity, and living in a state of permanent calm. This belief is not only unrealistic but counterproductive.

The human brain produces thousands of thoughts every day. Many of them are repetitive, random, or even contradictory. To expect that all negative or intrusive thoughts can be eliminated is to misunderstand how the mind works. Negative thoughts are not failures; they are signals. They often highlight fears, unmet needs, or unresolved issues. Suppressing them only strengthens their grip, much like trying to hold a beach ball underwater—it resurfaces with more force.

A more accurate picture of mental freedom is not the absence of negative thoughts but the ability to notice them without being controlled by them. For example, thinking "I might fail" is not the problem; believing that thought as absolute truth is. The skill lies in observing the thought, questioning its accuracy, and choosing whether to act on it.

In practice, mental freedom looks less like a silent mind and more like a spacious mind—one that can contain negativity without being overwhelmed by it.

Myth 2: Mental Freedom Requires Constant Positivity

Another widespread misconception is that to be mentally free, one must maintain a positive mindset at all times. This "good vibes only" culture has become pervasive, especially in online spaces. While positivity has benefits, forcing it can create a subtle form of self-rejection.

When people insist on constant positivity, they often deny or invalidate their real emotions. Sadness, anger, fear, or grief are labeled as "bad" emotions to be avoided. But emotions are not moral categories; they are data. Anger might point to injustice, sadness to loss, fear to caution. Each has a role in guiding action.

Research in emotional psychology shows that people who suppress difficult emotions tend to experience higher stress, poorer physical health, and lower overall well-being. Conversely, those who acknowledge and process emotions—even uncomfortable ones—develop greater resilience.

Mental freedom, therefore, is not about positivity at all costs. It is about authenticity. It means allowing yourself to feel the full range of human emotions, while still choosing how to respond to them.

Myth 3: Mental Freedom Is a Final Destination

Many people imagine mental freedom as a fixed state: once achieved, it remains forever. This belief creates frustration when old patterns resurface, leading individuals to conclude they have failed.

In reality, mental freedom is not a permanent destination; it is a practice. Just as physical fitness requires ongoing effort, mental clarity requires continuous attention. Life presents new challenges, losses, and transitions. Each brings opportunities for growth, but also the risk of falling back into old habits.

Someone who has worked through fear of rejection may feel free in relationships—until a new heartbreak reactivates old wounds. Someone who has cultivated calm may feel balanced—until a sudden crisis triggers anxiety. These moments do not mean freedom has been lost; they mean the practice must be renewed.

Understanding mental freedom as a process rather than an endpoint prevents discouragement. It shifts the goal from "arriving once and for all" to "learning how to return, again and again."

Myth 4: Mental Freedom Requires Complete Control Over the Mind

Some people equate freedom with absolute control: the ability to dictate every thought, emotion, or impulse. But control is not freedom; it is another form of rigidity.

The paradox is that trying to control the mind often creates more struggle. Imagine telling yourself, "Don't think about failure." Immediately, failure becomes the dominant thought. This phenomenon, known as the "ironic process" in psychology, shows that suppression backfires. The harder you try to control, the less free you become.

True mental freedom is not control but flexibility. It means allowing thoughts and feelings to arise, while retaining the ability to shift focus or perspective. A free mind is not a perfectly obedient servant—it is a responsive partner. It can wander, but it can also return. It can feel deeply, but it can also recover.

This flexibility is closer to resilience than control. Resilience does not demand perfection; it builds confidence that, whatever happens, you can navigate it.

Myth 5: Mental Freedom Means Freedom from Responsibility

Another subtle misconception is that mental freedom means escaping responsibility—detaching from obligations, pressures, or expectations. Some interpret freedom as doing whatever they want, whenever they want, without regard for others.

But genuine freedom is not avoidance. Avoiding responsibility often leads to more entrapment, not less. Bills still pile up, relationships suffer, and self-respect erodes. A life without responsibility is not freedom; it is chaos.

Instead, mental freedom comes from choosing responsibilities consciously, rather than being enslaved by unconscious patterns or external pressures. It is the difference between feeling forced to work late because of fear of judgment and choosing to work late because it aligns with your goals. In both cases, the action may be the same, but the internal experience is radically different.

Freedom is not the absence of responsibility; it is alignment between values and actions.

Myth 6: Mental Freedom Means Escaping the Past

It is tempting to believe that mental freedom requires erasing past pain. But the past cannot be erased; it can only be integrated.

Trying to "forget" difficult experiences usually makes them stronger, as unresolved emotions linger beneath the surface. Someone who insists, "The past doesn't matter," may unconsciously repeat its patterns because they have not truly faced it.

Mental freedom does not mean forgetting the past—it means reinterpreting it. It means seeing past events as part of your story, but not the whole story. It means acknowledging what was painful, extracting its lessons, and refusing to let it dictate the present.

As psychiatrist Viktor Frankl observed, suffering ceases to define us when we find meaning in it. The past shapes us, but mental freedom allows us to decide what role it will play in our future.

Myth 7: Mental Freedom Belongs Only to Certain People

Some believe mental freedom is reserved for monks, spiritual gurus, or people with extraordinary discipline. Ordinary individuals, weighed down by jobs, families, or financial pressures, are thought to be excluded.

This belief is dangerous because it discourages people from even trying. But history is filled with examples of individuals who cultivated freedom of mind under extreme circumstances. Nelson Mandela, imprisoned for 27 years, described how he preserved his dignity and hope through inner clarity. Holocaust survivors like Viktor Frankl wrote of finding meaning in unimaginable suffering.

If freedom can be nurtured in those conditions, it can certainly be nurtured in everyday life. Mental freedom is not about retreating from the world; it is about navigating it with awareness. It belongs not to the privileged few but to anyone willing to practice.

The Cost of Believing in Myths

Why do these myths matter? Because they create false expectations that lead to disappointment. When people assume mental freedom means constant positivity, they judge themselves harshly for feeling sad. When they assume it is a permanent state, they despair when old habits resurface. When they assume it requires total control, they exhaust themselves in endless self-battle.

These misconceptions add another layer of chains. Instead of working with the mind as it is, people chase an impossible standard. Ironically, the pursuit of these myths often creates more suffering than the challenges they were meant to solve.

The Reality: What Mental Freedom Truly Is

Stripped of myths, mental freedom is not about perfection, control, or escape. It is about awareness, choice, and alignment.

- **Awareness** means seeing thoughts and emotions clearly, without denial or distortion.
- **Choice** means recognizing that you are not bound to react automatically; you can respond intentionally.
- **Alignment** means living in accordance with values rather than being driven by fear, conditioning, or external pressure.

A free mind still has negative thoughts, still feels pain, and still encounters setbacks. The difference is that these experiences no longer dictate the entire reality. Freedom is not the absence of chains, but the recognition that many of them were illusions all along.

Takeaway: Clarity Over Illusion

Mental freedom loses its power when defined by myths. It is not endless positivity, not absolute control, not a final destination, and not the privilege of a chosen few. It is a practice—an ongoing process of awareness, choice, and alignment.

The key is to release the illusions that freedom means never struggling, never feeling, or never failing. When we let go of these myths, we stop chasing fantasies and begin practicing the kind of clarity that is possible here and now.

In that clarity, freedom is not distant—it is available in every present moment.

Identifying Your Personal Mental Blocks

Every person has unique barriers that keep their mind from experiencing clarity and freedom. These barriers, or mental blocks, act like invisible walls. They stop us from moving forward, drain our energy, and often leave us confused about why we feel stuck. Unlike external obstacles—financial limitations, physical challenges, or social circumstances—mental blocks are internal. They exist in thought patterns, beliefs, habits, and emotional reflexes.

The challenge is that mental blocks often remain hidden. They disguise themselves as "just the way I am" or "the reality of life." Because of this, people live for years within the confines of these invisible walls without realizing they are self-imposed. The path to mental freedom begins with identifying them. Awareness is the master key: what you can see, you can change.

What Mental Blocks Look Like

Mental blocks do not always announce themselves with dramatic symptoms. More often, they appear subtly in daily life. They show up as hesitation when opportunities arise, procrastination on important tasks, recurring self-doubt, or unexplained emotional triggers.

Some common signs include:

- **Avoidance:** Repeatedly putting off actions that align with your goals.
- **Self-Sabotage:** Engaging in behaviors that undermine success, such as procrastinating before deadlines or withdrawing in relationships.
- **Perfectionism:** Setting impossibly high standards, then feeling paralyzed by the fear of not meeting them.
- **Chronic Indecision:** Struggling to make choices, even small ones, due to fear of making the "wrong" move.

- **Emotional Overreaction:** Responding with disproportionate anger, fear, or sadness in situations that do not objectively warrant it.

Each of these patterns points to a deeper block beneath the surface. Recognizing these outer behaviors is the first clue in tracing the roots of what holds you back.

The Hidden Nature of Blocks

Why are mental blocks so hard to identify? Because they often feel like truth. If you believe you "just aren't good at relationships," you might not see this as a block—it feels like reality. If you constantly think, "I don't have time," you may not question whether it's a thought pattern or a genuine fact.

This hidden nature makes mental blocks more powerful than external barriers. A physical wall can be seen and climbed. A mental wall is invisible, so you may never attempt to cross it. The greatest challenge is not the block itself, but the unawareness of its presence.

The Most Common Categories of Mental Blocks

Though each person's blocks are unique, they often fall into several recognizable categories. Understanding these categories helps you recognize patterns in your own life.

1. Fear-Based Blocks
Fear is one of the strongest forces shaping mental barriers. Fear of failure, rejection, judgment, or uncertainty can stop progress before it begins. For example, someone may avoid public speaking, not because they lack skill, but because they fear embarrassment.

2. Belief-Based Blocks
These are rooted in limiting beliefs—deep-seated assumptions about yourself or the world. A belief like "I'm not smart enough" or

"People can't be trusted" acts as a filter, restricting choices and possibilities.

3. Habit-Based Blocks
Sometimes the block is not emotional but behavioral. Procrastination, distraction, or overconsumption of media create patterns that prevent clarity. The habit itself becomes the wall.

4. Identity-Based Blocks
These occur when your self-image conflicts with your goals. For instance, if you identify as "a shy person," you may resist opportunities that require confidence, even if you secretly desire them.

5. Trauma-Based Blocks
Past experiences, especially painful ones, can leave deep imprints that shape present behavior. Someone who experienced betrayal may struggle to trust, even when a relationship is safe.

By placing your blocks into these categories, you begin to map the architecture of your inner walls.

How to Spot Your Blocks in Daily Life

Identifying mental blocks requires deliberate reflection. Here are some practical approaches:

1. Track Patterns of Avoidance
Ask yourself: *What do I consistently avoid, even though I know it would benefit me?* The answer often reveals a block. For example, avoiding networking events may point to a fear of rejection.

2. Listen to Your Self-Talk
Your inner dialogue is one of the clearest indicators of blocks. Phrases like "I can't," "I always," or "That's just not me" reveal beliefs that may be limiting. Write down recurring phrases and examine them critically.

3. Observe Emotional Triggers

Notice when your emotional response feels bigger than the situation. A sharp criticism from a colleague may trigger extreme shame if it echoes childhood experiences of disapproval. Emotional overreactions are windows into hidden blocks.

4. Look at Recurring Life Themes

Do you repeatedly face the same problem in relationships, work, or personal growth? Patterns often indicate underlying blocks. For instance, repeated job dissatisfaction may reflect a belief about unworthiness or fear of pursuing true passion.

5. Ask Trusted Others

Sometimes blocks are easier to see from the outside. A trusted friend, mentor, or therapist can point out blind spots you overlook.

Real-World Examples

Consider Sarah, an entrepreneur who dreams of expanding her business but constantly delays launching new projects. At first, she tells herself she is "too busy." But deeper reflection reveals a fear of failure rooted in childhood criticism. The block is not lack of time—it is fear disguised as practicality.

Or take Michael, who longs for deeper relationships but pulls away whenever intimacy grows. He convinces himself he "just isn't relationship material." In reality, his block is a trauma-based belief formed after being abandoned in a past relationship. His present avoidance protects him from pain but also prevents connection.

These examples show that what looks like laziness, disinterest, or personality traits often masks deeper blocks.

Tools for Identifying Your Blocks

Practical exercises make the process of identification more concrete.

1. Journaling Prompts

- "What goals have I set repeatedly but failed to pursue? Why?"
- "What situations trigger the strongest fear or self-doubt in me?"
- "What beliefs about myself do I state as facts, even without evidence?"

2. Mind Mapping
Write down a recurring challenge, such as procrastination. Then draw branches asking "Why?" repeatedly. Often, the root emerges as a block: fear of imperfection, fear of judgment, or self-doubt.

3. Visualization
Close your eyes and imagine pursuing a goal. Notice where your mind resists. Does it say, "You're not capable"? Does your body tense? These reactions point to hidden blocks.

4. Cognitive Checklists
Use a list of common blocks (fear of failure, perfectionism, scarcity mindset, imposter syndrome) and check which resonate most with your experiences.

The Courage to Confront Blocks

Identifying mental blocks is not comfortable. It requires confronting fears, wounds, and self-deceptions. Many avoid this process because it feels easier to blame external circumstances. But without confronting blocks, freedom remains elusive.

Courage means admitting: *The wall is in my mind, not outside it.* This admission is not self-blame—it is empowerment. It means the power to change lies within you, not in waiting for the world to rearrange itself.

From Awareness to Action

Identifying a block is only the beginning. Once recognized, the block must be tested. If you believe, "I'm not creative," challenge it by engaging in small creative tasks. If you avoid conflict, test yourself by voicing a small opinion. Each action provides evidence that the block is not absolute.

Importantly, dismantling blocks takes time. Just as they were built through years of repetition, they dissolve through repeated challenges. The key is persistence—small steps, taken consistently, create cracks in the wall until it collapses.

The Role of Compassion in Identification

While identifying blocks, it is vital to approach yourself with compassion. Self-criticism only reinforces the very patterns you seek to break. Instead of saying, "I'm weak for having this block," say, "This block once protected me, but now it holds me back."

Every block was formed for a reason—to protect, to adapt, to survive. Compassion honors that past purpose while freeing you to move beyond it.

Takeaway: Awareness Unlocks the Door

Mental blocks are not flaws; they are learned patterns. They appear as avoidance, self-sabotage, indecision, or emotional overreaction. They are built from fear, belief, habit, identity, or trauma. And they remain powerful only as long as they remain unseen.

The first step to mental freedom is not demolishing every wall at once, but recognizing where the walls stand. With awareness, you can begin to test, challenge, and gradually dissolve them.

Mental freedom does not mean never facing blocks—it means developing the clarity to see them and the courage to step through them. Once identified, the invisible walls lose their power, and the path forward opens.

CHAPTER 2

Science of a Free Mind

Neuroscience of Thought Patterns

The mind often feels like an abstract space—a swirl of ideas, emotions, and images that seem to appear out of nowhere. But behind every thought is a concrete biological process. The brain, with its billions of neurons and trillions of connections, generates thought patterns that determine how we perceive, react, and decide. Understanding the neuroscience of thought patterns is not just an intellectual exercise; it is a key to freedom. When you grasp how your brain produces recurring thoughts, you begin to see why you get stuck, how habits form, and most importantly, how you can change them.

The Brain as a Network of Patterns

The human brain is not a static organ. It is a dynamic network constantly processing information, predicting outcomes, and creating meaning. Every thought you have—whether it is a memory, a fear, a creative idea, or a self-judgment—is the result of neurons firing in a specific pattern.

Neurons communicate through electrical signals and chemical messengers called neurotransmitters. When a thought occurs, thousands of neurons fire in sequence, forming a circuit. The more often a particular thought is repeated, the stronger the circuit becomes. This is why certain thoughts feel automatic—your brain has built well-worn pathways for them.

Imagine walking through a field of tall grass. The first time, the path is difficult to push through. But if you walk the same route repeatedly, a trail forms. Thoughts work the same way. Repeated thinking, whether positive or negative, creates stronger trails in the brain. These trails eventually become mental defaults.

The Default Mode Network: The Brain at Rest

One of the most important discoveries in neuroscience is the **default mode network (DMN)**. This is a set of interconnected brain regions that becomes active when the mind is not focused on a task—essentially, when you are daydreaming, reflecting, or wandering mentally.

The DMN is heavily involved in self-referential thinking: replaying memories, imagining the future, analyzing social interactions, and constructing your sense of self. While this network is essential for creativity and identity, it also fuels overthinking, rumination, and self-criticism.

For example, when the DMN is hyperactive, people often experience intrusive thoughts like, "Why did I say that?" or "What if I fail tomorrow?" This explains why the mind can feel restless even in moments of quiet. The brain does not shut off—it loops through patterns rooted in past experiences and future worries.

Understanding the DMN helps us see why mental freedom is not about stopping thought but about changing the relationship with thought. By recognizing when the brain is stuck in default rumination, we can learn to redirect attention toward constructive focus.

Neural Pathways and Habitual Thinking

Every recurring thought strengthens a neural pathway. This principle is summed up by a famous saying in neuroscience: *"Neurons that fire together wire together."* If you repeatedly think, "I am not good enough," the neurons supporting that thought become more efficient at firing together. Over time, the belief feels automatic and unquestionable.

The good news is that this process works both ways. Positive or empowering thoughts also strengthen neural pathways. When you repeatedly remind yourself, "I can learn this," you create new circuits that compete with old, limiting ones.

The challenge is that negative thought patterns often dominate because of the brain's **negativity bias**—its tendency to give more weight to threats and failures than to neutral or positive events. From an evolutionary perspective, this bias helped humans survive by keeping them alert to danger. But in modern life, it leads to an overemphasis on self-criticism and worry.

Memory and the Persistence of Patterns

Memories play a crucial role in shaping thought patterns. Each time you recall a memory, the brain reactivates the neural circuits associated with it. Interestingly, memory is not a static record; it is reconstructed each time. This means that revisiting a memory can reinforce it—or reshape it.

For example, someone who often recalls a past failure may strengthen a pattern of self-doubt. On the other hand, reframing the same memory—by focusing on what was learned rather than what was lost—can gradually shift the associated thought pattern.

This flexibility of memory is central to mental freedom. It shows that even long-held patterns are not fixed. By deliberately reinterpreting past experiences, we can weaken negative cycles and build new narratives.

The Role of Neurotransmitters

Thought patterns are not only about structure; they are also influenced by chemistry. Neurotransmitters—the brain's chemical messengers—play a key role in how thoughts feel and how sticky they become.

- **Dopamine** fuels motivation and reward. Positive anticipation strengthens circuits related to curiosity and drive.

- **Serotonin** influences mood and stability. Low serotonin levels are linked with repetitive negative thinking, while balanced levels support calm.
- **GABA (gamma-aminobutyric acid)** acts as an inhibitory signal, calming overactive neural circuits. Deficiencies can contribute to anxiety loops.
- **Glutamate** supports learning and memory, reinforcing circuits when experiences are repeated.

When neurotransmitter systems are imbalanced, thought patterns become skewed. For instance, low dopamine may leave someone stuck in apathetic loops, while excessive glutamate activity may intensify obsessive rumination. Understanding this biology reveals why mental patterns feel powerful—they are reinforced both structurally and chemically.

Thought Patterns and Emotional Hijacking

Thoughts are not isolated; they are tied to emotional circuits. When the amygdala detects a potential threat, it can hijack the brain's reasoning centers, producing fear-based thought loops. This is why anxiety often feels overwhelming: once the emotional system activates, rational thought is overshadowed.

For example, hearing criticism may trigger not just the thought, "I need to improve," but a cascade of fear-driven patterns: "I'm a failure. I'll lose my job. I'll never succeed." These catastrophic thoughts are not accurate predictions but products of an emotional hijack.

Recognizing when emotions are driving thought patterns allows us to pause and engage the prefrontal cortex—the part of the brain responsible for rational decision-making. This is where practices like mindfulness and breathing exercises become powerful tools; they calm the amygdala and restore balance between emotion and reason.

Real-World Illustration: The Cycle of Rumination

Consider Emily, a university student who often replays conversations in her head. After giving a presentation, she spends hours thinking, "I shouldn't have said that. They must think I'm stupid." Each recall strengthens the neural pathway of self-criticism. Her DMN remains hyperactive, feeding the loop.

The result is a cycle: thought triggers emotion (shame), which triggers more thought (self-doubt), which reinforces the original pattern. Over time, Emily begins to avoid public speaking, convinced she is incapable. Her behavior is shaped not by objective ability but by entrenched thought patterns.

This example shows how neuroscience explains everyday struggles. The brain is not broken—it is simply following the strongest pathways. The key to freedom is building new ones.

The Power of Neuroplasticity

The brain's most remarkable feature is **neuroplasticity**—its ability to reorganize itself by forming new connections. For centuries, scientists believed the adult brain was fixed. Now we know it changes continuously, even into old age.

Every time you learn something new, practice a skill, or change a thought, the brain rewires itself. Old pathways weaken through disuse, while new pathways strengthen through repetition. This means no thought pattern is permanent.

Neuroplasticity is the scientific foundation for hope. It proves that mental traps, no matter how entrenched, can be dismantled. The inner critic, the cycle of overthinking, the fear of failure—these are not destiny. They are patterns. And patterns can be changed.

Practical Implications: Shaping Thought Patterns

Understanding the neuroscience of thought patterns leads to actionable strategies:

1. **Interrupt the Loop** – When you notice a recurring negative thought, pause. Even a brief disruption prevents reinforcement of the old pathway.
2. **Replace, Don't Suppress** – Suppressing a thought strengthens it. Instead, introduce a new perspective. Shift "I'll fail" to "I'm learning, and progress is success."
3. **Repetition Builds Strength** – Consistently practicing new thoughts, affirmations, or reframes strengthens alternative pathways. Small daily practices have compounding effects.
4. **Use the Body to Influence the Brain** – Exercise, nutrition, and sleep directly affect neurotransmitters, creating conditions for healthier thought patterns.
5. **Practice Mindfulness** – Observing thoughts without judgment reduces DMN overactivity, allowing space between thought and reaction.

The Future of Thought Pattern Research

Emerging technologies like brain imaging and neurofeedback are giving scientists unprecedented insight into thought processes. Already, studies show that meditation physically alters brain structures, strengthening regions related to attention and emotional regulation. Cognitive training exercises are being developed to help people shift entrenched patterns faster.

As this field evolves, one truth remains: while biology sets the stage, experience rewrites the script. You are not merely the sum of your past thought patterns; you are capable of shaping the ones that come next.

Takeaway: Patterns Are Powerful, But Not Permanent

Thought patterns are the brain's way of making sense of the world. They are formed by repeated neural activity, reinforced by memory and chemistry, and shaped by emotion. Left unchecked, they can trap us in cycles of fear, doubt, and rumination. But neuroscience also offers profound hope: the same mechanisms that create patterns allow us to change them.

Mental freedom begins when we understand that thoughts are not facts—they are circuits. And circuits can be rewired. By practicing awareness, repetition, and conscious reframing, we can shift from being prisoners of old patterns to architects of new ones.

The Power of Neuroplasticity to Rewire Habits

When people talk about change, they often describe it as if it were a battle between willpower and resistance: a struggle to force themselves into new behaviors and away from old ones. But neuroscience reveals a different and more hopeful reality. The brain itself is designed to adapt. It is not fixed in structure or ability; it is dynamic, reshaping itself in response to experience. This remarkable capacity is called **neuroplasticity**, and it is the key to breaking old habits and creating new ones.

Understanding neuroplasticity changes how we approach personal growth. Instead of seeing ourselves as trapped by biology or history, we realize that every thought, action, and repetition is reshaping the architecture of the brain. Mental freedom is not a vague dream; it is a biological process that can be cultivated with intention.

What Neuroplasticity Really Means

Neuroplasticity is the brain's ability to form new neural connections and reorganize existing ones. For centuries, scientists believed the brain's wiring was mostly fixed after childhood. This belief implied that adults had little ability to change deeply ingrained habits or heal from trauma. But research in the late 20th and early 21st centuries overturned that view.

Today, we know that neuroplasticity operates throughout life. When you learn a new skill, practice a new habit, or think in a new way, the brain physically changes. Synapses—the junctions between neurons—strengthen or weaken depending on use. Areas of the brain can even shift functions if needed. For example, in blind individuals, regions of the brain normally devoted to vision can adapt to process sound and touch with heightened sensitivity.

This adaptability proves that change is not only possible but biologically natural. The question is not whether your brain can change—it is how you direct that change.

The Science of Habit Loops

To understand how neuroplasticity rewires habits, we must first understand how habits are structured. Psychologist Charles Duhigg describes habits as loops with three parts:

1. **Cue** – a trigger that initiates the behavior (e.g., stress, a time of day, a place).
2. **Routine** – the behavior itself (e.g., smoking, checking your phone, exercising).
3. **Reward** – the benefit the brain associates with the behavior (e.g., relaxation, distraction, satisfaction).

When a habit is repeated, the brain strengthens the neural pathway linking cue to routine to reward. Eventually, the behavior becomes automatic. This is why habits can feel so difficult to change: the brain has optimized itself for efficiency, favoring the familiar loop.

But neuroplasticity also makes change possible. By altering the routine or attaching a new reward to the same cue, we can gradually weaken old loops and build new ones. The brain does not erase old pathways overnight, but it can create competing ones that, with repetition, become dominant.

Real-World Example: Rewiring Procrastination

Take the case of Daniel, a graduate student who struggles with procrastination. Every time he sits down to study, he feels stress (cue). His automatic response is to check social media (routine). The reward is temporary relief from anxiety. Over time, this loop strengthens, and studying becomes increasingly difficult.

Using neuroplasticity, Daniel can rewire the loop. He recognizes the cue (stress), but instead of defaulting to social media, he introduces a new routine: two minutes of deep breathing followed by opening his notes. The reward shifts from avoidance to a sense of control. At first, the old loop is stronger. But each repetition of the new routine strengthens a new pathway. Over weeks and months, procrastination weakens, and focus grows.

This example illustrates how neuroplasticity is not an abstract concept; it is the biological basis for changing the habits that shape everyday life.

Repetition: The Architect of Change

The central principle of neuroplasticity is **repetition**. Each time a behavior or thought is repeated, the brain reinforces the neural pathway that supports it. The process is like forging a trail in a forest: the more times you walk the path, the clearer and easier it becomes.

This explains why habits, both good and bad, feel automatic. A smoker does not consciously decide each time; the pathway is so well-rehearsed that the brain defaults to it. But it also explains why deliberate practice builds skill. Musicians, athletes, and professionals strengthen their abilities by repeating precise actions until the neural circuits become highly efficient.

For anyone seeking mental freedom, this means small, repeated actions are more powerful than rare bursts of effort. Consistency rewires the brain; intensity without repetition does not.

The Role of Attention in Rewiring

Not all repetition creates change. Attention is the catalyst. Neuroscience research shows that when actions are performed with deliberate focus, they produce stronger neural changes than when performed mindlessly.

For instance, practicing gratitude mechanically ("I'm grateful for my coffee, my chair, my pen") may have limited impact. But pausing to truly reflect on a meaningful moment of gratitude—savoring the feeling—strengthens the neural circuits associated with positive emotion.

This insight reveals why mindfulness practices are so powerful: they train the brain to pay attention, making rewiring more efficient. Each time you bring conscious awareness to a thought or habit, you increase the brain's ability to reshape it.

Emotional Intensity and Lasting Change

While repetition is critical, emotionally intense experiences can accelerate neuroplasticity. The brain prioritizes memories and habits linked with strong emotions because they are more likely to be relevant for survival.

For example, a single traumatic event can leave a long-lasting imprint, creating a powerful negative habit of avoidance or fear. On the other hand, peak positive experiences—like achieving a meaningful goal or receiving deep affirmation—can strengthen circuits of confidence and motivation.

This explains why breakthroughs often occur during emotionally charged moments: a decision made in the midst of deep frustration or inspiration can catalyze lasting change. By pairing strong emotions with new habits (e.g., celebrating small wins with genuine excitement), we increase the brain's likelihood of wiring them in.

Breaking Old Habits: The Role of Synaptic Pruning

Just as the brain strengthens circuits through repetition, it also weakens unused ones through **synaptic pruning**. Pathways that are not activated regularly begin to fade. This is why habits you stop practicing eventually feel less automatic.

However, pruning takes time. Quitting an old habit does not erase the old pathway immediately. The brain still remembers it, which is why relapses are common. The key is persistence: the longer you go without activating the old loop, the weaker it becomes, while the new loop grows stronger.

Case Study: From Fear to Freedom

Consider Leah, who has a deep fear of speaking up in meetings. Every time she remains silent, her brain reinforces the belief that silence equals safety. The neural pathway of avoidance becomes stronger.

With coaching, Leah begins to rewire. Her cue (feeling anxious when called on) remains, but instead of silence, she practices stating one short comment. The first few attempts are shaky, but each time she experiences the reward of being heard without catastrophe. Gradually, the new pathway strengthens: anxiety cue → speaking → relief and confidence. Over months, her fear diminishes, and her participation grows natural.

This transformation is not magic; it is neuroplasticity at work.

Practical Strategies for Harnessing Neuroplasticity

1. **Start Small, Repeat Often**
   Large, dramatic changes are overwhelming for the brain. Micro-habits—tiny, consistent actions—are more sustainable. For example, instead of "I will meditate an hour daily," start with one minute. The repetition builds momentum.
2. **Pair New Habits with Existing Cues**
   Leverage established pathways by attaching new behaviors to familiar triggers. For example, after brushing your teeth (cue), practice one affirmation (routine). The brain associates the new habit with the old cue, making it easier to remember.
3. **Celebrate Progress**
   Reinforcement matters. By celebrating small wins with genuine enthusiasm, you flood the brain with dopamine, making the new habit more rewarding and more likely to stick.
4. **Visualize Success**
   Mental rehearsal activates many of the same neural circuits as real practice. Athletes use visualization to strengthen performance; anyone can use it to prepare the brain for new habits.
5. **Limit Competing Pathways**
   Reduce exposure to cues that trigger old habits. If you are rewiring a pattern of overeating, don't keep tempting foods in easy reach. This decreases the activation of old circuits, accelerating pruning.

Why Change Feels Hard at First

Many people abandon change because the beginning feels uncomfortable. This is not a sign of failure; it is neuroscience. When a new habit is first practiced, the old pathway is still stronger. The brain defaults to the familiar, even when it no longer serves you.

Think of it like switching from a paved highway to a dirt trail. At first, the highway is smoother and faster. But if you keep walking the trail, it becomes clearer over time. Eventually, the trail becomes the preferred path.

Understanding this process helps cultivate patience. The discomfort of starting is not a sign of impossibility—it is the natural friction of rewiring.

The Broader Implications of Neuroplasticity

The discovery of lifelong neuroplasticity reshapes how we view identity itself. If the brain can change, then personality, beliefs, and habits are not rigid traits but evolving patterns. This means that "I'm just not that kind of person" is rarely true. With practice and persistence, almost any skill or perspective can be cultivated.

This insight also reshapes how we view healing. Trauma and old wounds may leave deep imprints, but they do not have to define a person forever. With therapeutic interventions, supportive environments, and consistent practice, even the most entrenched patterns can be softened and replaced.

Takeaway: Freedom Is Built, Not Found

Neuroplasticity reveals that the brain is a builder. It constructs habits, beliefs, and identities through repeated practice. But it is also a renovator—it can dismantle old structures and create new ones.

Mental freedom is not about willpower alone; it is about working with the biology of the brain. By understanding habit loops, practicing repetition with attention, and embracing patience, you harness the natural plasticity of your mind.

The walls of old habits are not permanent. With each small, intentional action, you lay the bricks of a new pattern. Freedom is not discovered—it is built, one neural pathway at a time.

Stress and the Brain: Cortisol's Hidden Effects

Stress is an unavoidable part of human life. At times, it sharpens focus, fuels motivation, and prepares us for challenges. At other times, it feels like a heavy fog clouding judgment, draining energy, and creating endless worry. Behind this wide range of effects lies a single molecule with immense influence: **cortisol**, the body's primary stress hormone.

Understanding cortisol's role in the brain is crucial to mental freedom. Many people believe stress is only an emotional state—feeling tense, pressured, or overwhelmed. But stress is also a biochemical process that alters memory, decision-making, attention, and even the structure of the brain. These hidden effects explain why stress feels so pervasive and why mental clarity can vanish under pressure.

The Stress Response: A Survival Mechanism

To understand cortisol, we must first understand stress itself. Stress evolved as a survival mechanism. When our ancestors faced threats—a predator in the wild, a sudden storm—the brain triggered the **fight-or-flight response**. The amygdala signaled danger, the hypothalamus activated the adrenal glands, and the body flooded with adrenaline and cortisol.

This response prepared the body for action:

- Heart rate and blood pressure increased to supply muscles with oxygen.
- Blood sugar rose to provide quick energy.
- Non-essential functions, such as digestion, slowed down.
- The brain sharpened attention toward the threat.

For short-term dangers, this system was life-saving. After the threat passed, cortisol levels dropped, and the body returned to balance.

The problem arises when this system is activated too often or for too long. Modern stressors—deadlines, financial worries, traffic, social conflict—may not be life-threatening, but the brain reacts as if they are. As a result, cortisol remains elevated, and what was once protective becomes harmful.

Cortisol's Impact on the Brain

Cortisol is not inherently bad. In fact, small, short-term bursts improve alertness and memory. But chronic exposure to cortisol disrupts brain function in several critical ways.

1. Memory and Learning
Cortisol directly affects the hippocampus, the brain's memory center. In small doses, it enhances memory consolidation—this is why stressful events are often vividly remembered. But prolonged high cortisol damages hippocampal neurons, shrinking the region and impairing both memory and learning. This explains why people under chronic stress struggle to focus, retain information, or recall details.

2. Emotional Regulation
Cortisol also influences the amygdala, the brain's fear center. Chronic stress enlarges and overactivates the amygdala, making the brain hypersensitive to threats. As a result, individuals under stress perceive danger more often, even in safe situations. This fuels anxiety, irritability, and emotional overreactions.

3. Decision-Making
The prefrontal cortex, responsible for rational thought and self-control, is particularly vulnerable to cortisol. Elevated stress hormones reduce activity in this region, impairing judgment and increasing impulsivity. Under stress, people are more likely to make short-term decisions, avoid risks entirely, or default to familiar patterns—even if those patterns are unhelpful.

4. Creativity and Problem-Solving

High cortisol narrows attention, focusing the brain on immediate threats. While this tunnel vision is useful for survival, it suppresses creativity and flexible thinking. Chronic stress leaves little room for insight, innovation, or perspective. This is why solutions seem obvious after a stressful event has passed but impossible in the moment.

The Vicious Cycle of Stress

One of the most insidious effects of cortisol is that it creates a self-reinforcing loop. Stress alters the brain in ways that make it harder to cope with stress, which in turn raises cortisol further.

For example, chronic stress weakens the hippocampus, impairing memory. Forgetfulness then creates more stress, which further damages the hippocampus. Similarly, stress amplifies the amygdala, which increases sensitivity to threats, creating more stress signals.

This cycle explains why stress can feel endless. Without intervention, the brain becomes wired for stress, making relaxation and clarity increasingly difficult.

Real-World Illustrations

Consider Maya, a corporate manager juggling tight deadlines and constant meetings. At first, the stress motivates her, helping her stay alert and productive. But after months without real rest, she notices her memory faltering. She forgets appointments, struggles to recall names, and feels irritable with her team. Her brain, once sharp, now feels foggy. This is not laziness or incompetence—it is cortisol's effect on her hippocampus and prefrontal cortex.

Or take Alex, a student preparing for exams. Despite studying for weeks, on the day of the test his mind goes blank. Stress-induced cortisol has disrupted memory retrieval, leaving him unable to access what he knows. His struggle is not a lack of preparation but the biochemical hijacking of his brain.

These cases highlight a crucial truth: stress is not only psychological. It is physical and neurological, altering performance in ways that feel beyond conscious control.

Hidden Long-Term Effects

Beyond immediate cognitive changes, chronic cortisol exposure has lasting consequences for brain health.

- **Structural Shrinkage** – Long-term stress shrinks the hippocampus and prefrontal cortex while enlarging the amygdala.
- **Neurogenesis Suppression** – Cortisol reduces the birth of new neurons, limiting the brain's ability to adapt and rewire.
- **Accelerated Aging** – Chronic stress shortens telomeres, protective caps on DNA, contributing to cellular aging and cognitive decline.

These effects show that managing stress is not a luxury—it is a necessity for long-term mental freedom.

Stress, Identity, and Belief Loops

Cortisol does not just impair memory or judgment; it reinforces negative beliefs. When the brain is under stress, it favors efficiency over accuracy. This means it defaults to familiar thought patterns, even if they are limiting.

For example, someone who believes "I can't handle pressure" will, under stress, automatically replay that belief. The cortisol-fueled amygdala amplifies the fear, confirming the belief. The loop becomes self-fulfilling.

This is why chronic stress often strengthens limiting beliefs and negative self-talk. The brain under cortisol pressure is less capable of questioning assumptions and more likely to recycle old narratives.

Strategies for Managing Cortisol

The good news is that cortisol regulation is within our control. The brain and body have natural mechanisms for calming the stress response. By activating them deliberately, we can break the cycle and restore clarity.

1. Breathing Practices
Slow, deep breathing activates the parasympathetic nervous system, which lowers cortisol. Techniques like box breathing (inhale for 4, hold for 4, exhale for 4, hold for 4) can calm the body within minutes.

2. Physical Activity
Exercise reduces baseline cortisol levels and improves hippocampal growth. Even moderate movement, like walking, signals to the body that the stress response can subside.

3. Sleep
Cortisol follows a daily rhythm, peaking in the morning and declining at night. Sleep deprivation disrupts this cycle, keeping cortisol elevated. Prioritizing rest is one of the most powerful ways to restore balance.

4. Social Connection
Positive social interactions release oxytocin, which buffers cortisol's effects. Talking with trusted friends, engaging in community, or even physical touch can reduce stress responses.

5. Mindfulness and Meditation
Regular meditation has been shown to reduce amygdala activity and strengthen the prefrontal cortex, counteracting cortisol's effects. Even short daily sessions build resilience.

6. Nutrition
High-sugar diets can spike cortisol, while nutrient-rich diets (especially omega-3 fatty acids, magnesium, and vitamin B

complex) support regulation. Small dietary shifts create a biochemical environment for calm.

Case Study: Reclaiming Clarity

Ethan, a healthcare worker, experienced burnout after years of high-stress shifts. His memory suffered, his mood darkened, and his motivation collapsed. At first, he believed he was simply "weak" or "not cut out" for the job. But with guidance, he learned that his symptoms were cortisol-driven.

By integrating daily breathing exercises, consistent sleep, and weekend social activities, Ethan gradually lowered his baseline stress. Within months, his memory improved, his irritability decreased, and his sense of focus returned. The transformation was not a change of personality—it was the brain's natural recovery once cortisol was managed.

The Bigger Picture: Stress as a Teacher

While cortisol has destructive effects when chronic, it is not the enemy. Stress is a teacher. It signals when demands exceed resources, when rest is needed, or when boundaries are crossed. The goal is not to eliminate stress but to work with it consciously.

Mental freedom comes from recognizing that stress is both biological and psychological. By understanding cortisol's role, we stop blaming ourselves for struggles that are rooted in chemistry. Instead, we use practical tools to restore balance, creating conditions for clarity, focus, and resilience.

Takeaway: Mastering Cortisol for Mental Freedom

Stress is inevitable, but being controlled by it is not. Cortisol, the body's stress hormone, affects memory, decision-making, emotion, and creativity. In small bursts, it sharpens performance; in chronic doses, it erodes mental freedom.

The key is awareness and regulation. By practicing breathing, movement, sleep, connection, mindfulness, and nutrition, we harness the body's natural systems for balance. When cortisol is managed, the brain returns to clarity.

Freedom does not come from a stress-free life—it comes from mastering the stress response. In that mastery lies the power to think clearly, act intentionally, and live with resilience.

How Emotions Hijack Rational Thinking

Human beings like to imagine themselves as rational creatures. We pride ourselves on logic, reason, and the ability to make deliberate choices. Yet, if you examine daily life closely, you'll notice something surprising: many decisions are not guided by rational thought at all but by emotions. Whether it's the anger that drives a heated response, the fear that prevents a bold step forward, or the excitement that leads to impulsive action, emotions frequently take the driver's seat.

This phenomenon—emotions hijacking rational thinking—has deep roots in brain structure and evolution. It is not simply a flaw of character but a design of biology. Understanding how and why emotions override reason is vital for achieving mental freedom. Only by recognizing the hijack can we reclaim choice in moments of intensity.

The Evolutionary Role of Emotional Hijacks

From an evolutionary perspective, emotions evolved long before rational thinking. The limbic system—the emotional center of the brain—is millions of years older than the prefrontal cortex, the seat of logic and planning. In survival terms, emotions had to act fast. If our ancestors encountered a predator, stopping to logically weigh options would have been fatal. Fear needed to take over immediately, triggering the body to run or fight.

This evolutionary legacy explains why emotions can override logic so swiftly. The amygdala, the brain's alarm system, has a direct line to the body's stress response. When it detects potential danger, it can flood the system with stress hormones before the prefrontal cortex has time to analyze. This rapid response increases survival chances in true emergencies but often misfires in modern contexts. A critical email from a boss or an awkward silence in a meeting is not life-threatening, yet the brain reacts as if it were.

The Amygdala Hijack

Psychologist Daniel Goleman coined the term **"amygdala hijack"** to describe moments when emotions overwhelm rational thinking. During a hijack, the amygdala triggers an intense emotional response—anger, fear, or panic—before the rational brain can intervene. This is why you might say something in anger that you later regret, or freeze in fear despite knowing you are safe.

Once the amygdala hijack occurs, cortisol and adrenaline flood the body, narrowing focus and pushing logic aside. Blood flow shifts away from the prefrontal cortex, impairing reasoning, planning, and impulse control. The result is reactive behavior—fast, automatic, and often unhelpful in modern situations.

Everyday Examples of Emotional Hijacks

- **In Relationships**: A partner forgets to do a chore, and instead of calmly discussing it, the amygdala hijack triggers an outburst. Hours later, when calm returns, the person wonders, "Why did I overreact?"
- **At Work**: A manager offers constructive criticism, but the employee's emotional circuits interpret it as a threat. The hijack produces defensiveness, overshadowing the rational opportunity to learn.
- **In Decision-Making**: A stock market dip triggers panic, leading an investor to sell impulsively, even when rational analysis would recommend holding steady.

These examples illustrate that hijacks are not rare; they shape many everyday choices.

Why Rational Thinking Struggles Against Emotions

The reason emotions so easily dominate is that the emotional brain is faster and stronger in immediate response. Rational thinking requires more time and energy, while emotional circuits act instantly. Neuroscientists often say the emotional brain can "shout louder" than the rational brain, at least in the short term.

Additionally, emotions color the way we perceive reality. A fearful person will notice more threats; an angry person will see more injustices. Logic does not start from a neutral baseline—it is filtered through emotional states. This means that even when we believe we are reasoning, our conclusions may be shaped heavily by the emotions active at the time.

The Positive Side of Emotional Influence

It's important to note that emotional influence is not always negative. Emotions provide essential data for decision-making. Without them, reasoning can become paralyzed. In fact, studies of patients with damage to the emotional centers of the brain show that they struggle to make even simple choices, endlessly analyzing without a sense of preference or urgency.

Emotions highlight what matters. Joy signals alignment with values, anger highlights boundaries crossed, fear warns of potential danger. The problem is not that emotions exist—it is when they hijack control completely, leaving reason powerless.

The Role of Emotional Memory

Emotions are deeply tied to memory. The amygdala stores emotional experiences and uses them to interpret current events. This explains why reactions sometimes feel disproportionate. A mild criticism today may trigger a flood of shame rooted in childhood experiences. The brain does not distinguish clearly between past and present; it reacts as if old pain is happening again.

This emotional memory system helps us learn quickly—touching a hot stove once ensures we never repeat it. But it also means we carry emotional imprints that distort rational thinking long after the original event has passed.

Real-World Case Study: The Interview Freeze

Consider Lisa, a qualified candidate interviewing for her dream job. Despite preparing thoroughly, when the interviewer asks a challenging question, she blanks out completely. Her amygdala hijack interprets the question as a threat, flooding her with cortisol. Rational memory retrieval shuts down, leaving her unable to respond. Later, she remembers exactly what she wanted to say.

Lisa's experience was not incompetence; it was an emotional hijack. Recognizing this distinction is critical. Without understanding, she might form the limiting belief, "I'm terrible in interviews." With understanding, she can practice calming techniques that reduce hijacks in future interviews.

Strategies for Preventing Emotional Hijacks

1. **Pause Before Reacting**
   Even a few seconds can give the prefrontal cortex time to catch up. When triggered, take a slow breath before responding. This interrupts the hijack long enough for logic to re-engage.
2. **Name the Emotion**
   Labeling feelings ("I'm angry," "I'm anxious") activates the rational brain and reduces amygdala activity. This simple step helps shift from reaction to reflection.
3. **Reframe the Trigger**
   Ask: *Is this situation truly dangerous, or does it just feel that*

way? Reframing helps the brain distinguish between real threats and perceived ones.

4. **Practice Emotional Regulation Daily**
   Mindfulness, journaling, and breathing exercises train the brain to recover faster from hijacks. Like building a muscle, regular practice increases resilience.
5. **Strengthen the Prefrontal Cortex**
   Activities that demand focus and self-control—like meditation, learning new skills, or even puzzle-solving—enhance the prefrontal cortex, giving it more strength to counter emotional impulses.

Using Emotions Constructively

The goal is not to suppress emotions but to integrate them with reason. Instead of asking, "How do I stop feeling this?" a more powerful question is, "What is this emotion telling me, and how can I use it wisely?"

- Anger may signal a need to set boundaries. Rational thinking can then decide how to express those boundaries constructively.
- Fear may highlight risk. Rational analysis can then determine whether the risk is real or exaggerated.
- Excitement may signal opportunity. Rational planning can then ensure the opportunity is pursued wisely, not impulsively.

This integration transforms emotions from hijackers into allies.

The Long-Term Rewiring of Emotional Responses

Repeatedly practicing emotional regulation creates new neural pathways. Over time, the amygdala becomes less reactive, and the prefrontal cortex gains stronger control. This is neuroplasticity in action—emotions that once hijacked become manageable signals.

For example, someone who practices public speaking repeatedly, while calming themselves, gradually reduces the fear response. The amygdala learns that the situation is not life-threatening, and rational thinking remains accessible even under pressure.

Takeaway: Freedom Between Emotion and Reaction

Emotions will always influence thinking—they are too ancient and powerful to be erased. But mental freedom is not about eliminating emotions; it is about mastering the space between emotion and reaction.

By understanding the amygdala hijack, recognizing emotional memory, and practicing regulation, we prevent emotions from seizing control. Instead, we allow logic and feeling to work together.

In this balance lies true clarity: emotions provide energy and meaning, while rational thinking provides direction. Mental freedom emerges not from silencing emotion, but from ensuring it serves rather than dominates.

Mind-Body Connection: Why Clarity Begins Inside

When people speak about mental clarity, they often imagine it as purely a function of the mind—something achieved through sharper focus, better thinking, or stronger willpower. But neuroscience, psychology, and physiology tell a different story: the mind does not exist in isolation. It is inseparably linked to the body. The state of your body—your posture, breath, hormones, gut health, and nervous system—directly shapes the state of your mind.

This is the essence of the **mind-body connection**: the recognition that what happens in the body influences thought, emotion, and decision-making, and vice versa. Mental fog, anxiety, or lack of focus are not simply "mental problems." They are often the byproduct of physical imbalances. Likewise, cultivating physical practices—movement, breathing, nutrition, sleep—creates conditions where clarity, calm, and freedom become possible.

To understand mental freedom fully, we must explore why clarity begins not only with thought but with the body that generates thought.

The Nervous System: The Bridge Between Body and Mind

The nervous system acts as the communication highway between body and mind. It transmits signals about internal states (hunger, fatigue, stress) and external events (threats, opportunities) to the brain. These signals shape thoughts and emotions more than most people realize.

Two key branches of the nervous system are central to the mind-body connection:

- **Sympathetic Nervous System (SNS):** Activates the fight-or-flight response. It mobilizes energy in response to stress or danger.
- **Parasympathetic Nervous System (PNS):** Activates the rest-and-digest response. It promotes recovery, calm, and restoration.

When the SNS dominates, the body is in survival mode: muscles tense, heart rate accelerates, and the brain narrows focus to potential threats. Mental clarity is reduced because resources are devoted to immediate survival. When the PNS is active, the body relaxes, digestion improves, and the brain opens space for reflection and creativity.

This explains why practices like deep breathing, yoga, or meditation are so effective: they activate the PNS, restoring balance and creating a physiological foundation for clarity.

The Gut-Brain Axis: Your "Second Brain"

Another surprising link between body and mind lies in the gut. The digestive system contains over 100 million neurons—so many that scientists call it the "second brain." These neurons communicate with the central nervous system through the vagus nerve, influencing mood, energy, and focus.

Research shows that gut bacteria produce neurotransmitters like serotonin, dopamine, and GABA, which affect emotional regulation. In fact, about 90% of serotonin—the neurotransmitter most associated with well-being—is produced in the gut.

This means that diet and gut health have a direct impact on mental clarity. Diets high in processed foods, sugar, and unhealthy fats can disrupt gut bacteria, leading to inflammation and mood instability. Conversely, nutrient-rich foods, probiotics, and fiber support a healthy gut microbiome, which in turn supports a healthy mind.

Clarity truly begins inside—sometimes as literally as what you eat for breakfast.

Hormones and Mental States

Beyond the gut, hormones throughout the body shape thought patterns and emotions. Cortisol, as we saw earlier, influences stress. But other hormones also play critical roles:

- **Insulin:** Regulates blood sugar. Sharp spikes and crashes can create mood swings, fatigue, and brain fog.
- **Thyroid Hormones:** Affect metabolism and energy. Imbalances can lead to lethargy or anxiety.
- **Estrogen and Testosterone:** Influence mood, confidence, and motivation. Fluctuations can create shifts in emotional stability.

Many people blame themselves for lack of focus or emotional swings when, in reality, their physiology is at play. By understanding and regulating hormones—through lifestyle, medical care, or stress reduction—mental clarity becomes far more attainable.

Movement as Medicine for the Mind

Physical movement is one of the most direct ways to influence the mind. Exercise increases blood flow to the brain, delivering oxygen and nutrients that fuel cognition. It also stimulates the release of brain-derived neurotrophic factor (BDNF), a protein that supports the growth of new neurons and neural connections.

Studies consistently show that regular physical activity improves memory, focus, and emotional regulation. Even moderate exercise, like brisk walking, reduces symptoms of anxiety and depression. Movement signals to the body that it is safe and capable, which translates into mental resilience.

Importantly, exercise need not be extreme to impact mental clarity. A short daily routine of stretching, walking, or light strength training is enough to shift the nervous system and elevate mood.

Breath: The Fastest Route to Calm

Breath is the most immediate tool for influencing the mind-body connection. Unlike other bodily functions, breathing is both automatic and controllable. This gives it unique power: by consciously changing breath patterns, we can change the body's signals to the brain.

For example:

- **Shallow, rapid breathing** signals danger, activating the sympathetic nervous system.

- **Slow, deep breathing** signals safety, activating the parasympathetic nervous system.

Breath practices like diaphragmatic breathing, box breathing, or alternate-nostril breathing have been shown to lower cortisol, calm the amygdala, and improve focus. These techniques demonstrate that clarity is not only about controlling thoughts—it begins with controlling the rhythm of the body.

Posture and Body Language

The way we hold our body also shapes the way we think. Research in embodied cognition shows that posture and facial expression feed back into emotional states. Slouching can increase feelings of fatigue or sadness, while upright posture promotes confidence and alertness.

In one study, participants who held "power poses" (open, expansive postures) reported feeling more confident and performed better in stressful situations. Though later research questioned the hormonal effects, the psychological impact remains clear: the body cues the brain about how to feel.

This means that changing your physical stance—standing tall, breathing deeply, moving with intention—can create a shift in mental clarity almost instantly.

Sleep: The Foundation of Mental Clarity

No factor demonstrates the mind-body connection more powerfully than sleep. During sleep, the brain consolidates memories, clears metabolic waste, and resets emotional circuits. Lack of sleep disrupts attention, problem-solving, and emotional regulation.

Research shows that even one night of poor sleep increases amygdala reactivity by up to 60%, making the brain more prone to emotional hijacks. Chronic sleep deprivation reduces prefrontal cortex function, impairing judgment and self-control.

Despite this, many people sacrifice sleep for productivity, not realizing that clarity and performance are being eroded at the foundation. Prioritizing sleep is not indulgence—it is the single most effective way to restore mental freedom.

Real-World Example: The Stressed Executive

Consider Olivia, an executive who struggles with constant brain fog and irritability. She assumes the problem is mental weakness and pushes herself harder at work. But a closer look reveals the truth: she sleeps only five hours a night, consumes mostly processed food, and rarely exercises. Her nervous system is stuck in sympathetic dominance, her gut health is compromised, and her cortisol levels are elevated.

When Olivia begins improving her sleep, adding daily walks, and shifting her diet, the fog lifts. Her memory improves, her emotions stabilize, and her focus sharpens. The transformation comes not from more willpower but from aligning body and mind.

Integrating Body Practices Into Mental Clarity Work

To cultivate mental freedom, practices that address the body must be integrated alongside cognitive strategies. Some practical steps include:

1. **Morning Movement:** Begin the day with light stretching or walking to energize the nervous system.
2. **Mindful Eating:** Choose foods rich in nutrients and supportive of gut health—whole grains, vegetables, probiotics, lean proteins.
3. **Scheduled Breathing Breaks:** Every few hours, pause for 2–3 minutes of slow breathing to reset cortisol levels.
4. **Sleep Hygiene:** Create consistent sleep routines, reduce evening screen time, and keep the bedroom dark and cool.
5. **Posture Awareness:** Set reminders to sit or stand upright, open the chest, and release tension.

6. **Daily Reflection:** Notice how physical states—hunger, fatigue, tension—affect mental clarity. Use this awareness to make adjustments.

The Deeper Lesson: The Mind Is Embodied

The greatest misunderstanding about mental clarity is the belief that the mind floats above the body. In reality, the mind is embodied. Thought is not separate from physical state; it emerges from it.

This perspective shifts how we approach mental freedom. Instead of fighting the mind with more thoughts, we learn to care for the body that generates them. When the body is balanced, the mind naturally becomes clearer. When the body is neglected, even the sharpest reasoning feels foggy.

Takeaway: Clarity Begins in the Body

The path to a free mind does not start only in the mind. It begins in the body—through the nervous system, the gut, the breath, the posture, and the rhythms of rest and movement. Clarity is not simply thinking better; it is living in a way that aligns body and brain.

By recognizing the inseparable link between body and mind, we gain new tools for freedom. Instead of struggling endlessly with thoughts, we cultivate the physical foundation that makes clear thinking possible. In this alignment, clarity is not forced—it flows naturally from within.

CHAPTER 3

The Art of Letting Go

Detachment Without Indifference

Letting go is one of the most misunderstood practices in personal growth. Many people assume that letting go means not caring, withdrawing from life, or abandoning ambition. They fear that detachment is the same as indifference: a cold disengagement from relationships, goals, or emotions. But true detachment is very different.

Detachment does not mean giving up on what matters; it means releasing the grip of unhealthy attachment. It is the practice of engaging fully with life—relationships, work, growth—without being enslaved by the outcomes. Far from indifference, detachment allows for deeper presence, clearer perspective, and greater freedom.

To live with detachment is to hold life with open hands: committed yet not controlling, caring yet not clinging. This subtle balance is one of the most powerful paths to mental clarity.

The Difference Between Detachment and Indifference

Indifference is a lack of care. It is disengagement, numbness, or apathy. When someone is indifferent, they stop investing energy because nothing seems to matter. It is a form of withdrawal—a retreat from life's richness.

Detachment, by contrast, is not about disengagement but about perspective. It is the ability to care deeply without being consumed. A detached person loves fully but does not collapse if rejected. They work diligently but do not tie their worth entirely to success. They feel emotions but do not let emotions dictate every choice.

This distinction is critical. Indifference diminishes life, while detachment enriches it. Indifference numbs, detachment liberates.

Why Attachment Creates Suffering

To understand detachment, we must first understand attachment. Attachment is not simply love or connection; it is the emotional fusion of identity and outcome. It is when you feel your sense of self depends entirely on whether something goes your way.

For example:

- "If this relationship ends, I will be nothing."
- "If I don't get this promotion, I am a failure."
- "If people don't like me, I am unworthy."

Attachment creates suffering because it ties internal peace to external events. Since life is unpredictable, external conditions can never be guaranteed. The more tightly we cling, the more fragile we feel.

This is not to say we should not have desires, goals, or relationships. The problem is not in wanting but in over-identifying. Detachment is the practice of separating identity from outcomes—of realizing, *I am whole regardless of what happens.*

The Neuroscience of Clinging

From a neurological perspective, attachment is reinforced by dopamine, the brain's reward chemical. When we anticipate or achieve something we want—praise, recognition, affection—the brain releases dopamine, reinforcing the behavior. Over time, this creates a craving loop.

Just as with addictive substances, the brain can become dependent on external validation or specific outcomes for a sense of satisfaction. When the outcome does not appear, dopamine drops, creating distress. This is why attachment feels so gripping—it is wired into reward pathways.

Detachment interrupts this loop. By shifting focus from outcome to process, from craving to presence, the brain learns to find satisfaction in engagement itself rather than in the uncertain arrival of a reward.

Real-World Illustration: The Artist and the Audience

Consider an artist who paints with deep passion. At first, she creates because she loves the process. Over time, as her work gains attention, she begins to feel pressure: *Will people like my next piece? Will this one get recognition?* The joy of painting shifts into anxiety about reception.

This is attachment at work. Her sense of identity becomes tied to audience approval. If the response is positive, she feels validated. If it is negative, she feels worthless.

Detachment would not mean she stops caring about her art. It would mean returning to the love of creation itself. She can still share her work, still value feedback, but her sense of self is no longer chained to applause. This frees her to create with authenticity rather than fear.

The Emotional Freedom of Detachment

Detachment creates emotional space. When you are detached, you can feel without being consumed. Anger arises, but you observe it instead of exploding. Fear appears, but you recognize it as a passing state rather than absolute truth. Joy comes, and you savor it without clinging desperately to keep it.

This emotional space is what psychologists call **response flexibility**—the ability to choose rather than react automatically. Detachment enhances resilience because it prevents emotions from hijacking reason. You are not suppressing emotions, nor are you enslaved by them. You are free to engage wisely.

Detachment in Relationships

Relationships are often the most difficult arena for detachment. Love easily becomes entangled with possession, control, or dependency. Many people equate detachment with coldness: "If I detach, won't I stop caring about the people I love?"

In truth, detachment allows for healthier love. When you are overly attached, you may try to control your partner, fearing loss. You may tolerate mistreatment because your identity feels bound to the relationship. Detachment, however, allows you to love without losing yourself. You can give freely, but you also know you remain whole if the relationship ends.

A detached person does not love less—they love more purely. Their care is not based on control but on presence and choice. They are free to support, nurture, and connect without fear-driven clinging.

Detachment in Work and Goals

Ambition often fuels attachment. Many people tie their worth to achievements: promotions, income, recognition. While goals are valuable, over-attachment creates constant anxiety: *What if I fail? What if I lose my edge? What if others surpass me?*

Detachment at work does not mean becoming unmotivated. It means shifting from outcome-obsession to process-engagement. A detached worker still strives for excellence but is not shattered by setbacks. They see failure as feedback, not as identity. They celebrate success without making it their sole source of worth.

Ironically, this detachment often increases performance. When pressure is reduced, creativity flows more freely, and risks are taken more confidently. Detachment is not the death of ambition—it is its liberation.

The Spiritual Dimension of Detachment

Across spiritual traditions, detachment is seen as a path to peace. Buddhism teaches that clinging is the root of suffering. The Bhagavad Gita emphasizes action without attachment to results. Stoic philosophy advises focusing on what is within control and releasing what is not.

In all these traditions, detachment is not withdrawal but alignment. It is about living fully, acting with integrity, and letting go of what cannot be controlled. The consistent message is that peace comes not from external certainty but from internal freedom.

Practical Strategies for Cultivating Detachment

1. **Awareness of Clinging**
   Notice where your identity feels tied to outcomes. Ask: *If this doesn't go my way, do I feel worthless?* Awareness is the first step to loosening the grip.
2. **Shift Focus from Outcome to Process**
   Instead of obsessing over results, concentrate on the quality of your actions. For example, focus on writing a strong essay rather than worrying about the grade.
3. **Practice Non-Attachment Language**
   Change phrases like "I need this" to "I prefer this." The subtle shift reduces psychological dependency.
4. **Daily Reflection**
   Ask yourself: *What am I clinging to today?* Write it down, then consciously remind yourself: *I am whole regardless of this outcome.*
5. **Meditation on Impermanence**
   Reflect on the transient nature of events and emotions. This builds perspective, reminding you that both joy and pain are temporary.
6. **Set Boundaries in Relationships**
   Healthy detachment includes knowing where you end and another person begins. Boundaries protect both connection and individuality.

7. **Engage Fully, Release Gracefully**
   When pursuing goals, give your best effort. When the outcome arrives—whether success or failure—practice letting go. This rhythm builds resilience.

Case Study: The Athlete's Mindset

James, a competitive runner, once defined himself by his victories. Every race became a test of identity. If he won, he felt valuable; if he lost, he spiraled into despair. His performance suffered under the weight of pressure.

Through coaching, James learned detachment. He began focusing on the discipline of training and the joy of running itself. Victories still mattered, but they no longer defined him. As his anxiety decreased, his performance actually improved. Detachment freed him to compete with clarity rather than fear.

Takeaway: Freedom Through Open Hands

Detachment is not coldness, laziness, or indifference. It is the art of caring deeply without clinging destructively. It is loving without losing yourself, striving without being consumed, and feeling without being enslaved.

Mental freedom requires this balance. Without detachment, life is a constant cycle of clinging and suffering. With detachment, you remain open, resilient, and free.

Clarity begins when you learn to hold life with open hands—engaged, caring, present, yet free from chains of unhealthy attachment.

Releasing Toxic Relationships and Influences

Few things shape the quality of your inner world as much as the people and environments around you. Relationships can be sources of growth, encouragement, and resilience—or they can be sources of stress, self-doubt, and limitation. The company you keep is not just social; it is psychological. Every interaction either feeds clarity or clouds it.

Yet, many people remain entangled in toxic relationships or environments long after recognizing their harm. Why? Because walking away is difficult. It stirs guilt, fear, obligation, and doubt. But learning to release what poisons the mind is a vital step toward inner freedom.

This section explores how toxic influences take hold, why they are so hard to let go of, and how to release them with clarity and compassion.

What Makes a Relationship Toxic?

Not every conflict or disappointment makes a relationship toxic. Healthy connections involve disagreements, challenges, and occasional frustration. Toxicity, however, is different. A toxic relationship consistently drains, manipulates, or undermines rather than supports growth.

Common markers of toxic relationships include:

- **Consistent Negativity:** The person criticizes, belittles, or shames more than they support.
- **Manipulation and Control:** They guilt-trip, gaslight, or coerce you into compliance.
- **Emotional Drain:** You feel exhausted, anxious, or diminished after interacting with them.

- **Lack of Reciprocity:** You give far more than you receive, often at the expense of your well-being.
- **Violation of Boundaries:** Your limits are ignored, dismissed, or ridiculed.

These signs are not about occasional mistakes; they are about persistent patterns. Over time, such relationships erode self-worth and clarity, chaining the mind in cycles of confusion and doubt.

The Psychology of Staying

If toxicity is so harmful, why do people stay? The reasons are often complex, rooted in psychology and emotion.

1. **Familiarity Bias**
   The human brain prefers the familiar, even when it is harmful. This is why people can feel strangely "comfortable" in unhealthy dynamics—they echo old, ingrained patterns.
2. **Fear of Loneliness**
   For many, the idea of being alone feels scarier than remaining in a toxic relationship. The fear of emptiness outweighs the pain of toxicity.
3. **Hope for Change**
   People often hold onto potential: "Maybe they'll change," or "It wasn't always this bad." This hope can keep them stuck, even when evidence suggests otherwise.
4. **Guilt and Obligation**
   Family ties, long histories, or cultural expectations can create pressure to endure toxicity rather than release it.
5. **Erosion of Self-Esteem**
   Toxic influences often chip away at confidence, convincing the person they don't deserve better or that leaving is impossible.

Understanding these psychological traps is the first step toward breaking free. They are not signs of weakness but reflections of how deeply human beings crave connection and belonging—even at great cost.

The Subtle Forms of Toxicity

Not all toxic influences are obvious. Some are subtle, dressed in care or disguised as humor. Recognizing them requires attentiveness.

- **Backhanded Support:** "I'm happy for you, but don't get too cocky."
- **Conditional Kindness:** Support given only when it benefits them.
- **Constant Comparison:** Highlighting how others are "better" or "smarter."
- **Energy Vampires:** People who constantly complain or offload negativity without interest in solutions.

Such dynamics may not feel overtly abusive but can quietly drain clarity and confidence over time.

Environments as Influences

Toxicity does not only come from individuals—it can come from environments. A workplace built on fear, gossip, or unrealistic demands can be just as damaging as a toxic friend. Media consumption also shapes mental clarity. Constant exposure to negativity, outrage, or unrealistic standards can warp self-perception and heighten anxiety.

Identifying toxic environments is as important as identifying toxic people. Both influence thought patterns, often in invisible ways.

Real-World Case Study: The Loyal Friend

Consider Daniel, who maintains a long-standing friendship with Mark. Over the years, Mark frequently belittles Daniel's choices, dismisses his accomplishments, and pressures him into unhealthy behaviors. Daniel often feels drained after spending time together but stays because "we've been friends since childhood."

This loyalty, though admirable, keeps Daniel locked in a cycle of doubt and negativity. Once he recognizes that history does not justify harm, he begins to set boundaries and reduce contact. As the influence weakens, Daniel notices his confidence rising. He realizes the loyalty he owed most was to himself.

The Process of Releasing

Letting go of toxic influences is rarely a single act. It is often a gradual process involving several stages:

1. **Recognition**
   The first step is acknowledging the harm. This may require journaling, therapy, or honest reflection. Denial keeps the cycle alive.
2. **Boundary Setting**
   Before cutting ties, many relationships can be tested with clear boundaries: "I won't tolerate being spoken to that way." The response reveals whether change is possible.
3. **Detachment**
   If boundaries are ignored, emotional detachment becomes necessary. This does not mean hostility; it means refusing to tie self-worth to the relationship.
4. **Separation**
   Sometimes, the healthiest choice is reducing or ending contact. This step may feel painful, but it creates space for healthier influences to enter.
5. **Healing**
   Releasing toxicity often brings grief. Even harmful relationships can hold memories of care or comfort. Healing requires acknowledging both the loss and the liberation.

Compassionate Release

Releasing does not always mean condemnation. Recognizing someone as toxic does not require labeling them as evil. Many toxic behaviors come from unhealed wounds, fear, or insecurity.

Compassion allows release without bitterness: *I choose not to carry this influence, but I wish them healing in their own journey.*

Compassionate release prevents resentment from becoming a new form of attachment. It ensures that letting go is truly freeing, not simply another chain.

Practical Tools for Releasing Toxic Influences

1. **Journaling for Clarity**
   Write about how you feel before, during, and after interactions. Patterns of drain or uplift become clearer on paper.
2. **Boundary Scripts**
   Prepare simple phrases to use in difficult conversations:

- "I'm not comfortable with that."
- "I need some space right now."
- "This isn't healthy for me, and I have to step back."

3. **Gradual Distance**
   If cutting ties feels too abrupt, reduce interaction gradually—fewer calls, less availability.
4. **Replace with Healthy Influences**
   Empty space must be filled. Seek communities, friends, or mentors who uplift, support, and challenge you constructively.
5. **Therapeutic Support**
   Professional guidance can provide strength and perspective, especially when family or long-term ties make release complex.

When Release Is Not Possible

Sometimes, complete release is not realistic—such as with coworkers, family, or community obligations. In these cases, detachment and boundaries become even more crucial. You may not control their behavior, but you control the degree of access they have to your emotions. Protect your inner clarity by limiting exposure and refusing to internalize their negativity.

Reclaiming Energy After Release

Once toxic influences are released, many people report an unexpected surge of energy. The mental bandwidth once consumed by negativity becomes available for creativity, joy, and growth. This is not just psychological—it is physiological. Stress hormones decline, sleep improves, and the nervous system regains balance.

The release itself is not only an act of removal but an act of reclamation: reclaiming time, energy, and clarity for what truly matters.

Takeaway: Choosing Freedom Over Familiarity

Toxic relationships and influences can quietly imprison the mind, eroding clarity and self-worth. Releasing them is not abandonment or betrayal—it is an act of alignment with freedom.

The process begins with recognition, continues through boundaries and detachment, and culminates in compassionate release. Along the way, courage is required to choose freedom over familiarity, clarity over comfort.

When you let go of what drains you, you create space for what nourishes you. Mental freedom is not just an inner practice; it is also a social choice. By releasing toxicity, you declare: *My clarity matters, my freedom matters, and my life will be shaped by influences that uplift rather than diminish.*

How to Stop Clinging to Outcomes

Human beings are goal-driven by nature. We set intentions, pursue dreams, and work toward achievements. This drive can be a source of progress and meaning. But when attachment to outcomes becomes rigid—when our sense of worth, happiness, or peace depends entirely on how things turn out—we begin to suffer.

Clinging to outcomes creates anxiety in the present, disappointment in the future, and a perpetual sense of lack. Even when we achieve what we desire, the satisfaction fades quickly, replaced by a new outcome to chase. Mental freedom requires a shift: learning to pursue goals with commitment but without unhealthy attachment to results.

Stopping the cycle of clinging is not about apathy or lowering standards. It is about engaging fully in effort while releasing the illusion of control over what cannot be controlled.

Why We Cling to Outcomes

The tendency to cling arises from both evolutionary design and cultural conditioning.

Evolutionary Roots
The brain evolved to seek reward and avoid loss. Dopamine fuels anticipation, creating a surge of motivation when a potential reward is in sight. This system was adaptive when rewards meant survival— food, shelter, safety. But in modern life, it drives us to fixate on achievements, recognition, and possessions as if they were matters of life and death.

Cultural Conditioning
Society reinforces outcome obsession. From grades in school to promotions at work, success is measured by results. Media glamorizes achievements while downplaying the process that

produced them. The message is clear: your worth is tied to what you accomplish.

Together, these forces make clinging feel natural. Yet, natural does not mean healthy.

The Psychological Cost of Clinging

Clinging to outcomes carries hidden costs that accumulate over time.

1. **Anxiety in the Present**
   When worth is tied to outcomes, every step toward them is filled with pressure: *What if I fail? What if I fall short?* Instead of enjoying the process, the mind is consumed by fear of the future.
2. **Disappointment in the Future**
   Even when outcomes are achieved, satisfaction is short-lived. Psychologists call this the **hedonic treadmill**—the tendency to adapt quickly to new achievements and immediately crave more.
3. **Loss of Presence**
   Clinging shifts attention away from the present moment into imagined futures. This creates a sense of restlessness, as though life is always "on hold" until the next milestone is reached.
4. **Distorted Identity**
   When identity is tied to results, failure becomes catastrophic: "If I fail, I am worthless." This fragile identity leads to avoidance of risk and stunted growth.

Real-World Case Study: The Entrepreneur

Consider Alex, a young entrepreneur launching a startup. His entire identity is wrapped up in the success of the business. Each day, instead of focusing on building value, he obsessively checks metrics, compares himself to competitors, and worries about failure. Even small setbacks feel crushing.

When Alex finally secures investors, his relief is brief. Almost immediately, he shifts to worrying about the next milestone. His joy is never in the present—it is always contingent on the next outcome. Over time, his health declines, and his creativity suffers.

Alex's struggle illustrates how clinging traps us in perpetual dissatisfaction, even when we "win."

Detachment from Outcomes vs. Apathy

It's important to clarify that detachment from outcomes is not the same as apathy. Apathy is disengagement, a refusal to care. Detachment, by contrast, is full engagement without enslavement.

An apathetic student says, "I don't care about the exam, so I won't study."
A detached student says, "I will study diligently, but I know my worth is not defined by the grade."

Apathy diminishes effort. Detachment preserves effort but releases unhealthy dependence on results. This is the mindset that fuels resilience and freedom.

Shifting Focus: From Outcome to Process

The most effective way to stop clinging is to shift focus from outcome to process. The process is what you can control—your actions, intentions, and presence. The outcome is influenced by countless variables outside your control—market shifts, others' choices, random chance.

By rooting identity in the process rather than the result, you free yourself from anxiety. Effort becomes meaningful in itself. Whether the outcome is success or failure, the process provides growth.

For example:

- A writer can focus on the joy of crafting words rather than obsessing over bestseller lists.
- An athlete can focus on training and discipline rather than solely on winning medals.
- A professional can focus on serving clients with excellence rather than fixating only on promotions.

Tools for Letting Go of Outcomes

1. Set Intentions, Not Attachments
Instead of saying, "I must get this promotion," reframe as: "My intention is to give my best at work and grow." This language shift emphasizes effort, not dependency on result.

2. Practice "If-Then" Detachment
Tell yourself: "If this outcome happens, I will celebrate. If it does not, I will still learn and grow." Both paths are valuable.

3. Use Process-Oriented Goals
Replace goals like "lose 10 pounds" with "exercise three times per week." The latter focuses on controllable actions, reducing anxiety.

4. Meditate on Impermanence
Reflect on how every outcome, whether success or failure, is temporary. This reduces the illusion that outcomes define permanent identity.

5. Journal the Circle of Control
Draw two circles: one for what you can control (effort, choices, attitude) and one for what you cannot (others' opinions, random chance). Review regularly to anchor focus on the first circle.

6. Celebrate Micro-Wins
Detach from distant results by celebrating small process victories: showing up, trying again, learning something new.

The Role of Acceptance

Detachment from outcomes requires acceptance. Acceptance does not mean resignation—it means recognizing reality as it is rather than as we demand it to be. By accepting uncertainty, we reduce the grip of fear. By accepting failure as part of growth, we prevent it from shattering identity.

Acceptance creates resilience. When outcomes are uncertain, acceptance ensures peace remains steady.

Emotional Freedom Through Letting Go

When you stop clinging to outcomes, something remarkable happens: you experience freedom in the present. Anxiety diminishes because the future is no longer a tyrant. Joy increases because the process itself becomes rewarding. Identity strengthens because it is no longer tied to fragile results.

This does not mean you abandon ambition. It means you pursue it from a place of wholeness rather than desperation. Paradoxically, this mindset often increases success. When pressure decreases, performance improves. When identity is secure, risks can be taken more boldly.

Real-World Example: The Musician

Sophia, a musician, once tied her self-worth entirely to winning competitions. Each performance became unbearable pressure, and mistakes haunted her. After working with a mentor, she shifted focus to the joy of music itself. She still competed, but her identity no longer hinged on results.

Ironically, her performances improved. Freed from crippling anxiety, she played with authenticity and passion. Her artistry blossomed when she stopped clinging.

A Philosophical Perspective

Ancient wisdom traditions echo this principle. The Bhagavad Gita teaches: *"You have the right to the work, but not to the fruits thereof."* Stoic philosophy emphasizes focusing only on what is within control. Buddhism teaches that clinging is the root of suffering. Across traditions, the message is consistent: peace lies not in outcomes but in how we engage with them.

Practical Reflection Exercise

Each evening, ask yourself:

1. *What did I focus on today that was within my control?*
2. *What outcomes am I clinging to, and how can I release them?*
3. *How did I grow today, regardless of results?*

Over time, this practice rewires the mind to value process over outcome.

Takeaway: Effort Without Chains

Clinging to outcomes enslaves the mind in cycles of anxiety, disappointment, and fragile identity. Freedom comes not from abandoning goals but from releasing dependency on results.

The art is in holding outcomes lightly—pursuing them with effort and passion while remembering they do not define your worth. Success and failure both become teachers, not prisons.

When you stop clinging, you rediscover joy in the journey. The path itself becomes meaningful, and freedom is no longer postponed until some future result—it is available here and now.

The Psychology of Forgiveness

Forgiveness is one of the most misunderstood yet transformative practices for mental freedom. Many people view forgiveness as weakness—an act of excusing harm, condoning injustice, or letting others "off the hook." Others see it as something owed only when an offender apologizes or changes. But forgiveness, as psychology and neuroscience reveal, is less about others and more about freeing ourselves.

Unforgiveness—the holding on to resentment, anger, or bitterness—acts like a mental anchor. It chains the present to the past, consuming emotional energy and clouding clarity. Forgiveness, in contrast, is not about forgetting or excusing; it is about releasing the emotional grip of harm so that the mind can reclaim peace.

Understanding the psychology of forgiveness helps us see it not as moral obligation but as a practical tool for mental clarity and resilience.

Why Forgiveness Is So Difficult

Forgiveness challenges us because it collides with natural instincts and deeply held beliefs.

1. The Justice Instinct
Human beings have a built-in sense of fairness. When wronged, the brain activates circuits associated with reward at the thought of revenge. This explains why "getting even" can feel temporarily satisfying. Forgiveness feels counterintuitive because it goes against this instinct for balance.

2. The Pain of Betrayal
When harm comes from someone we trusted, the wound cuts deeper. Betrayal challenges not only the event itself but also our perception of safety and identity. Forgiveness feels like letting go of the only shield we have against repeated pain.

3. Fear of Repetition

Many resist forgiveness because they fear it will invite more harm: "If I forgive, won't they just hurt me again?" This fear confuses forgiveness with reconciliation, though the two are not the same.

4. Identity and Victimhood

Sometimes, holding on to anger provides a sense of identity: "I am the one who was wronged." Letting go feels like losing part of oneself. Forgiveness requires stepping into a new identity—one not defined by injury.

What Forgiveness Really Is

Psychology defines forgiveness as a conscious decision to release resentment toward someone who has caused harm, regardless of whether they deserve it. It does not mean forgetting, excusing, or reconciling. It means refusing to let the past dictate emotional well-being in the present.

In this sense, forgiveness is less about the offender and more about the forgiver. It is the act of reclaiming power over your own mind by no longer carrying the weight of anger and bitterness.

The Neuroscience of Forgiveness

Studies using brain imaging reveal that forgiveness is not just a moral concept—it has biological effects. When people recall grudges, brain regions associated with stress and threat (the amygdala and insula) activate strongly. When people practice forgiveness, activity shifts toward brain regions linked with empathy and problem-solving (the prefrontal cortex and anterior cingulate cortex).

This shift reduces cortisol, lowers blood pressure, and activates the parasympathetic nervous system, promoting calm. Forgiveness literally changes the body's stress response, creating conditions for clarity.

The Psychological Benefits of Forgiveness

1. **Reduced Anxiety and Depression**
   Unforgiveness is linked with chronic stress, which fuels
   anxiety and depression. Forgiveness reduces rumination—the
   mental replay of harm—which is one of the strongest
   predictors of emotional distress.
2. **Improved Relationships**
   While forgiveness does not always mean reconciliation, it
   often improves existing relationships by breaking cycles of
   retaliation and resentment.
3. **Greater Resilience**
   Forgiveness builds the ability to recover from setbacks. By
   releasing attachment to past harm, the mind gains more
   flexibility to engage with present challenges.
4. **Enhanced Self-Esteem**
   When we forgive, we affirm our own worthiness of peace.
   We stop defining ourselves by wounds and reclaim agency
   over identity.

Real-World Case Study: The Estranged Siblings

Maria and Elena, sisters, had a falling out over inheritance disputes.
For years, Maria carried deep resentment, replaying the betrayal in
her mind. Each thought of Elena triggered anger and bitterness. Even
when not directly interacting, Maria's mental space was consumed.

Eventually, Maria worked with a therapist who helped her see that
forgiveness did not mean reconciling or pretending the betrayal was
acceptable. It meant choosing not to carry the emotional weight
anymore. Over time, Maria practiced reframing: "Her actions hurt
me, but my peace is my responsibility."

Though Maria and Elena never reconciled, Maria felt lighter. The
resentment that once dominated her thoughts lost power.
Forgiveness freed her mind even while boundaries remained intact.

The Distinction Between Forgiveness and Reconciliation

One barrier to forgiveness is the belief that it requires rebuilding a relationship. In reality, forgiveness and reconciliation are separate processes:

- **Forgiveness** is internal: the decision to release resentment.
- **Reconciliation** is external: the rebuilding of trust and connection.

Forgiveness can happen without reconciliation. You can forgive someone and still choose not to let them back into your life. This distinction is liberating: it allows for healing even when the other person never apologizes or changes.

How to Cultivate Forgiveness

Forgiveness is not a one-time event but often a gradual process. Here are key practices:

1. Acknowledge the Hurt
Forgiveness begins with honesty. Suppressing pain prevents healing. Acknowledge what happened and how it affected you.

2. Separate Person from Action
Recognize that harmful actions often arise from ignorance, insecurity, or pain. This perspective does not excuse behavior but humanizes the offender, making forgiveness possible.

3. Reframe the Story
Ask: *What meaning can I take from this experience?* Many find strength, resilience, or clarity in the lessons learned.

4. Practice Empathy (with Limits)
Empathy does not mean condoning harm. It means considering the context of the other's actions. This widens perspective and loosens the grip of resentment.

5. Use Forgiveness Rituals
Writing unsent letters, practicing guided meditations, or visualizing release can provide symbolic closure.

6. Repeat the Choice
Forgiveness is rarely final on the first attempt. Resentment may resurface. Each time, the choice can be repeated: *I release this again.*

When Forgiveness Feels Impossible

Some harms cut so deep that forgiveness feels unattainable. In these cases, it helps to reframe forgiveness not as a gift to the offender but as a gift to yourself. Even if you cannot imagine reconciliation or empathy, you can still release the power of the event over your mind.

Therapy, community support, and spiritual practices can assist in these cases. Sometimes forgiveness is less about a dramatic transformation and more about gradually reducing the intensity of anger until peace becomes possible.

The Role of Self-Forgiveness

Often, the hardest person to forgive is ourselves. Many carry guilt, shame, or regret for past mistakes, replaying them endlessly in the mind. Self-forgiveness is essential to mental freedom because self-condemnation keeps us trapped in cycles of avoidance or self-sabotage.

Self-forgiveness involves the same principles: acknowledging the mistake, separating self-worth from the action, extracting lessons, and releasing self-punishment. It does not mean ignoring responsibility; it means taking responsibility without perpetual self-condemnation.

Forgiveness as Strength

Far from being weakness, forgiveness requires immense strength. It demands facing pain honestly, releasing the intoxicating pull of resentment, and choosing peace over vengeance. Anyone can cling to anger; it takes courage to let it go.

Forgiveness is an act of reclaiming power. Instead of being defined by the wound, you define yourself by resilience. Instead of carrying the weight of bitterness, you walk lighter.

Takeaway: Freedom Through Release

Forgiveness is not about others—it is about your freedom. Unforgiveness chains the mind to past harm, distorting clarity and consuming energy. Forgiveness severs that chain. It does not erase the past or demand reconciliation; it reclaims the present.

By understanding the psychology of forgiveness—its challenges, distinctions, and practices—we gain a tool of profound liberation. Forgiveness is not forgetting, excusing, or weakening. It is choosing peace, clarity, and freedom over bitterness.

In the end, forgiveness is not about who deserves it. It is about who deserves peace—you.

Practical Exercises for Emotional Release

Understanding concepts like detachment, forgiveness, and letting go is powerful, but intellectual knowledge alone does not bring freedom. To truly release emotions, one must practice. Emotional release is a skill—a way of training the mind and body to process, express, and let go of feelings rather than storing them or letting them control us. Without release, emotions linger in the nervous system, resurfacing as stress, anxiety, or reactivity. With release, emotions become fluid experiences, passing through instead of getting stuck.

This section offers practical, science-backed exercises for emotional release. These practices are not abstract—they are daily tools that anyone can use to transform the way they engage with inner life.

Why Emotional Release Matters

The human tendency is to either suppress emotions or be consumed by them. Suppression buries emotions, creating tension in the body and unresolved mental loops. Overindulgence magnifies emotions, keeping the mind trapped in cycles of anger, fear, or sadness. Release provides the middle path. It allows emotions to be acknowledged, expressed, and then let go, restoring clarity and balance.

Research shows that unprocessed emotions contribute to chronic stress, which elevates cortisol, damages memory, and increases risk of physical illness. Conversely, healthy emotional expression improves resilience, strengthens relationships, and enhances overall well-being. Emotional release is not indulgence—it is hygiene for the mind.

Exercise 1: The Body Scan and Release

The body holds emotions. Anger may tighten the jaw or fists, fear may tense the stomach, sadness may weigh on the chest. The first step to release is awareness of these signals.

Practice:

1. Sit or lie down in a quiet space.
2. Close your eyes and take slow breaths.
3. Starting at the top of your head, scan down through the body, noticing areas of tension.
4. When you locate tension, breathe into that area. On the exhale, consciously soften.
5. Imagine releasing the stored energy with each breath.

This practice trains the mind to locate where emotions reside in the body and to release them physically.

Exercise 2: Journaling for Emotional Clarity

Writing externalizes emotions, moving them from the mind into visible form. This creates distance and allows for new perspective.

Practice:

1. Set a timer for 10–15 minutes.
2. Write continuously about what you are feeling without editing.
3. Use prompts such as: "I am angry because…," "What I fear is…," "What I need right now is…"
4. When the timer ends, either keep the journal for reflection or ritually discard the page (shred, burn, recycle) to symbolize release.

Studies show expressive writing reduces stress, improves immune function, and enhances mental clarity.

Exercise 3: The Release Breath

Breath is the fastest way to shift emotional state. The "release breath" emphasizes long exhalations, signaling safety to the nervous system.

Practice:

1. Inhale through the nose for four counts.
2. Exhale through the mouth for six to eight counts, as if sighing.
3. Repeat for several minutes, focusing on releasing tension with each exhale.

This technique is particularly effective for releasing anxiety, frustration, or restlessness.

Exercise 4: The Empty Chair Technique

Developed in Gestalt therapy, the empty chair technique provides a safe way to express unresolved emotions toward another person without confrontation.

Practice:

1. Place an empty chair in front of you.
2. Imagine the person you are addressing is sitting there.
3. Speak freely, expressing emotions you've held back. Say everything you need to, without censoring.
4. Switch roles if desired—sit in the other chair and respond as if you were them.

This practice helps release unspoken anger, grief, or resentment, even if the relationship itself cannot be resolved.

Exercise 5: Physical Expression of Emotion

Emotions are physical energy. Sometimes words are not enough—movement is required.

Practice:

- For anger: Punch a pillow, stomp feet, or engage in intense physical exercise.
- For sadness: Allow yourself to cry fully without judgment.
- For restlessness: Dance or shake out the body to release excess energy.

These practices may feel uncomfortable at first but provide profound relief. Suppressed emotion often lingers in the body until expressed physically.

Exercise 6: Visualization Release

The mind responds powerfully to imagery. Visualization can create symbolic closure that the body interprets as real.

Practice:

1. Close your eyes and imagine the emotion as an object—a heavy stone, a dark cloud, a locked box.
2. Visualize yourself placing it down, letting it float away, or dissolving it into light.
3. Affirm: "I release this now. I no longer need to carry it."

This exercise is especially useful for letting go of resentment or repetitive negative thoughts.

Exercise 7: Gratitude Reframing

Gratitude shifts focus from what was lost or painful to what is present and valuable. It does not erase pain but balances perspective.

Practice:

1. List three things you feel grateful for in the moment.
2. For each, pause and feel the gratitude in your body.
3. If the emotion is tied to a painful memory, ask: "What did this teach me? What strength did I gain?"

Gratitude reframing helps release the tight grip of negative emotions by broadening the lens of awareness.

Exercise 8: Sound Release

The voice is a natural tool for expression. Sound carries emotion outward.

Practice:

- Humming or chanting to release anxiety.
- Yelling or groaning into a pillow to release anger.
- Singing to express sadness or joy.

Sound vibration resonates through the body, loosening emotional tension.

Exercise 9: Forgiveness Rituals

When emotions are tied to resentment, forgiveness rituals provide closure.

Practice:

1. Write a letter to the person who hurt you, expressing everything you feel.
2. End with: "I release this pain. I choose peace."
3. Do not send the letter—destroy it to symbolize release.

This ritual combines expression with symbolic action, creating emotional closure.

Exercise 10: Daily Micro-Releases

Release is not only for big emotions. Small stresses build up daily and require regular clearing.

Practice:

- At the end of each day, take five minutes to reflect: "What tension am I carrying? What can I release right now?"
- Pair with breath, stretching, or journaling.

These micro-releases prevent accumulation and keep the mind clear.

Real-World Case Study: The Grieving Parent

After losing her father, Clara carried unresolved grief for years. She avoided crying, fearing it would overwhelm her. Instead, she developed anxiety and insomnia. Through therapy, she began practicing physical expression (crying fully in safe spaces), journaling, and forgiveness rituals. Gradually, her anxiety lifted. The grief did not vanish, but it flowed rather than stagnated. Clara discovered that emotional release did not erase love—it honored it.

Why Practice Matters

Emotional release must be practiced regularly, just like physical exercise. Suppressed emotions accumulate silently, only surfacing when triggered. Release prevents this build-up, keeping the emotional system flexible and resilient.

Think of emotional release as unclogging pipes. Without release, pressure builds until it bursts. With regular release, emotions flow smoothly, and clarity remains intact.

The Role of Compassion in Release

Emotional release must be accompanied by compassion. Many resist release because they judge themselves for feeling: "I shouldn't be angry," "I should be stronger." Compassion allows emotions to exist without shame. It says: "It's human to feel. I release because I deserve peace."

This self-compassion transforms release from an act of weakness into an act of strength.

Takeaway: Release as Daily Freedom

Emotional release is not a one-time event—it is a daily practice of hygiene for the mind. Through breath, writing, movement, visualization, sound, and ritual, emotions are allowed to flow rather than stagnate. This flow restores clarity, resilience, and peace.

Mental freedom does not come from suppressing emotions or drowning in them. It comes from the ability to release—acknowledging, expressing, and letting go with compassion. When practiced daily, emotional release becomes not just a technique but a way of living: a rhythm of clarity that keeps the mind free.

CHAPTER 4

Focus, Flow & Mental Energy

Why Multitasking Destroys Clarity

In today's world, multitasking is celebrated as a badge of productivity. Many people boast about juggling emails, meetings, social media, and household chores all at once. The modern workplace often expects employees to switch between projects rapidly, while digital culture encourages constant notifications, updates, and interactions. The illusion is that doing more at the same time means achieving more. Yet neuroscience tells a very different story.

Far from making us efficient, multitasking drains clarity, fragments focus, and reduces the quality of everything we do. The human brain is not designed to perform multiple high-level tasks simultaneously. Each switch between tasks carries a hidden cost: lost time, increased stress, and reduced mental energy. True clarity requires not more multitasking but the courage to focus deeply on one thing at a time.

The Myth of Multitasking

The word "multitasking" itself is misleading. Computers can multitask because they have parallel processors that run multiple operations at once. Human brains, however, do not have the same architecture. When we believe we are multitasking, what we are actually doing is rapid task-switching. The brain shifts attention back and forth, creating the illusion of simultaneous action.

This distinction is critical. Task-switching is not free—it comes with what psychologists call a **switching cost.** Each time the brain moves from one task to another, it requires time and energy to reorient. Even small switches—like checking a notification in the middle of writing—can derail focus. Studies show it can take the brain up to 20 minutes to fully return to the same level of concentration after an interruption.

The Neuroscience of Focus and Switching

To understand why multitasking destroys clarity, we must examine how attention works. The brain's prefrontal cortex, located just behind the forehead, is responsible for focus, planning, and decision-making. When concentrating on one task, the prefrontal cortex aligns neural resources toward that activity.

But when a new task appears, the brain must shift networks. This shift uses glucose and oxygen—the brain's energy currency. Frequent switching depletes resources, leaving the brain fatigued. Over time, this constant switching trains the brain to prefer distraction, making deep focus more difficult.

Neuroscientists have found that multitasking increases activity in the **anterior cingulate cortex,** the region that handles conflict monitoring. This means the brain is constantly juggling competing signals, which creates mental stress even if we do not consciously feel it.

The Productivity Illusion

Many people multitask because it feels productive. Answering emails during a meeting, checking messages while cooking, or scrolling social media between work tasks gives the impression of efficiency. But research shows the opposite: multitasking reduces productivity by up to 40%. The apparent speed is canceled out by errors, lower quality, and the time lost to reorienting.

One study by Stanford University found that heavy multitaskers performed worse on tests of attention and memory compared to light multitaskers. They struggled to filter irrelevant information and had reduced ability to switch tasks effectively. In short, those who multitasked most frequently were least skilled at managing multiple streams of information.

The Emotional Toll of Multitasking

Multitasking does not only affect productivity—it affects emotional well-being. Constant switching creates a sense of being perpetually rushed, even when no urgent deadline exists. It fuels anxiety because the mind is always split, never fully present.

Over time, this fragmented attention erodes satisfaction. When focus is divided, even enjoyable activities lose depth. Watching a movie while checking emails, for instance, diminishes the immersive pleasure of the film and reduces comprehension of the emails. Nothing is fully experienced; everything is half-lived.

Real-World Case Study: The Distracted Student

Consider David, a university student studying for exams. He believes he is being efficient by listening to lectures while scrolling through social media and texting friends. Yet, when tested, he retains little of the material. His study sessions stretch longer because each distraction requires him to re-engage with the material. David's anxiety grows because, despite hours spent "studying," he makes little progress. His problem is not lack of intelligence but lack of clarity, drained by multitasking.

The Myth of "Good Multitaskers"

Some people insist they are "good multitaskers." While individual differences exist, the research consensus is clear: the human brain is limited in processing multiple complex tasks. What some perceive as multitasking skill is usually rapid switching in areas where tasks are simple or automatic. For example, walking while talking is manageable because walking is largely automated by the brain. But combining two demanding tasks, like writing an email while participating in a meeting, inevitably reduces quality.

The Role of Technology in Fragmentation

Digital devices amplify multitasking. Smartphones, with their constant notifications, encourage micro-distractions that fracture focus. Social media platforms are designed to hijack attention, creating compulsive checking. Even the presence of a phone on a desk—silent and unused—has been shown to reduce cognitive performance, as part of the brain remains occupied with resisting the potential distraction.

This technological environment normalizes fragmented attention. Many people no longer realize how deeply multitasking erodes their clarity because they have never experienced extended deep focus.

The Cost to Mental Energy

Every decision, every switch, every act of resisting distraction consumes mental energy. Psychologists call this **decision fatigue.** When energy is depleted, self-control weakens, errors increase, and emotions run higher. Multitasking accelerates this depletion, leaving less energy for meaningful work, relationships, or creativity.

This explains why many feel exhausted after a day of fragmented attention despite accomplishing little. The brain is not tired from focused work—it is drained from constant switching.

Breaking the Multitasking Habit

Recognizing the cost of multitasking is the first step; the next is cultivating single-task focus. Here are practical strategies:

1. Time Blocking
Dedicate specific blocks of time to single tasks. For example, set 90 minutes for focused writing, then a short break, then a block for emails. This prevents overlap and preserves energy.

2. Eliminate Distractions
Silence notifications, close unnecessary tabs, and create a physical environment that reduces interruptions. Out of sight often means out of mind.

3. Use the "One Tab Rule"
Limit yourself to one active window or document at a time. This forces the brain to stay aligned on the current task.

4. Practice Mindfulness
Mindfulness trains attention to return gently to the present. Regular practice strengthens the brain's ability to resist distraction.

5. Celebrate Completion
Each finished task provides a sense of satisfaction. Acknowledge completions to reinforce the reward of single-tasking.

6. Start Small
If deep focus feels difficult, begin with 10–15 minutes of uninterrupted work. Gradually extend the duration as the brain adapts.

Real-World Case Study: The Focused Professional

Emma, a project manager, once prided herself on multitasking—juggling calls, emails, and meetings simultaneously. Yet her projects consistently ran behind, and her stress levels soared. After learning about the cost of multitasking, she began practicing time blocking, dedicating mornings to deep work and afternoons to meetings. Within weeks, her productivity and clarity improved. She discovered that by doing less at once, she accomplished more overall.

The Deeper Lesson: Depth Over Breadth

The modern world rewards speed and quantity, but mental freedom requires depth and quality. Multitasking scatters attention across breadth—many shallow engagements. Single-tasking concentrates attention into depth—one meaningful engagement.

Depth leads to mastery, satisfaction, and clarity. Breadth without depth leads to exhaustion and confusion. The choice is not about doing everything at once but about doing the right things fully.

Takeaway: One Thing at a Time

Multitasking destroys clarity because the brain is not built for simultaneous complex tasks. Each switch fragments attention, drains energy, and diminishes satisfaction. The path to freedom lies in reclaiming focus—doing one thing at a time with full presence.

When you resist the lure of multitasking, you rediscover the richness of attention. Work becomes more effective, relationships more meaningful, and life more vivid. Clarity begins not with doing more, but with focusing on less.

Building Single-Task Focus in a Noisy World

If multitasking scatters clarity, then single-tasking restores it. Yet, in our modern environment, cultivating single-task focus is not simple. We live in what psychologists call an "attention economy," where countless forces compete for mental space. Notifications, advertisements, conversations, and demands from work and home create an endless stream of distractions. In such a noisy world, focusing on one task at a time requires more than good intentions—it requires strategy, discipline, and environmental design.

Single-tasking is the practice of directing attention toward one meaningful activity with full presence. It is not merely doing less; it is doing differently. Instead of fragmenting attention across multiple demands, single-tasking channels it fully, producing higher quality, deeper satisfaction, and greater mental freedom.

Why Single-Tasking Feels Difficult

Many people try to single-task only to find their attention wandering. This difficulty is not personal weakness—it is the result of brain wiring and external conditioning.

1. Dopamine and Novelty
The brain craves novelty. Each time you switch tasks or check a notification, dopamine provides a small reward. Over time, the brain becomes conditioned to seek these mini-rewards, making sustained focus feel boring or uncomfortable.

2. Conditioned Distraction
Technology and media train the brain for short attention spans. Scrolling social media, flipping between apps, and consuming rapid-fire information make deep focus unfamiliar.

3. Fear of Missing Out (FOMO)
Single-tasking often feels risky because it means ignoring other tasks or notifications. The fear of missing something important pulls attention away from the present task.

4. Internal Noise
Even in silence, the mind generates distractions—worries, memories, to-do lists. Without training, the mind resists stillness, making it harder to remain focused.

Recognizing these challenges is important. Focus is not automatic in a noisy world—it is a skill that must be cultivated intentionally.

The Neuroscience of Deep Focus

When we single-task, the brain engages the prefrontal cortex and sustains activation in task-specific networks. Over time, repeated focus strengthens these neural pathways, making concentration easier.

But when we constantly switch tasks, the brain strengthens circuits for distraction. This is why people who multitask often find it difficult to focus, even when they try. Attention, like a muscle, strengthens in the direction it is trained.

Single-tasking also engages the brain's **flow state**—a condition of deep immersion where time feels suspended and performance peaks. Flow is impossible in multitasking because it requires sustained attention on one challenge.

The Benefits of Single-Task Focus

1. **Higher Productivity**
   Focusing on one task reduces errors and eliminates switching costs. Work is completed more efficiently and with greater accuracy.
2. **Greater Creativity**
   Deep focus allows the brain to form new connections. Creativity emerges not from fragmented attention but from immersion.
3. **Reduced Stress**
   Single-tasking lowers cognitive load. Instead of juggling, the brain relaxes into one stream of action, reducing anxiety.
4. **Deeper Satisfaction**
   Full presence in one activity increases fulfillment. Whether working, conversing, or relaxing, the experience feels richer.

Real-World Case Study: The Overloaded Employee

Samantha, a marketing manager, constantly juggled emails, phone calls, and reports. Her days felt frantic, and despite long hours, progress was slow. Frustrated, she began practicing single-tasking. She blocked two hours each morning for deep work, silenced notifications, and set her phone aside. Within weeks, she noticed not only higher productivity but also greater calm. Her evenings felt lighter because tasks were completed with focus rather than scattered effort.

Practical Strategies for Building Single-Task Focus

1. Design Your Environment
Environment shapes behavior. Reduce external noise by silencing devices, decluttering the workspace, and using headphones or quiet spaces when possible. Out of sight is often out of mind.

2. Use Time-Blocking
Schedule tasks in dedicated blocks of time. For example, 9–11 a.m. for writing, 1–2 p.m. for emails. Time-blocking creates mental boundaries, reducing the temptation to juggle.

3. Apply the Pomodoro Technique
Work for 25 minutes with full focus, then take a 5-minute break. This trains the brain to focus in manageable intervals while preventing fatigue. Over time, the intervals can be extended.

4. Create a "Not Now" List
When distractions arise, jot them down on a list instead of acting on them. This assures the mind that they won't be forgotten, freeing attention for the current task.

5. Train with Mindfulness
Mindfulness meditation strengthens attention by repeatedly bringing the mind back to the present. Even 10 minutes a day can improve single-task focus.

6. Start with Rituals
Create a ritual that signals focus time—lighting a candle, playing specific music, or making tea. Over time, these rituals train the brain to shift into concentration more easily.

7. Limit Task Switching Windows
Instead of checking email throughout the day, designate two or three specific times. This reduces the constant drain of micro-distractions.

The Role of Boundaries

Single-task focus often requires setting boundaries with others. Colleagues, friends, and even family may expect constant availability. Communicating clearly—"I'm offline for the next two hours, but I'll respond after"—protects focus while maintaining connection. Boundaries transform focus from a personal struggle into a shared understanding.

Internal Focus Training

External strategies help, but internal training is also vital. The wandering mind is the greatest source of distraction. Training involves building tolerance for stillness and resisting the urge to switch.

One simple practice is **single-point attention**: choose one small object, such as a candle flame or a breath, and keep attention there. Each time the mind wanders, gently return. Over time, this builds the ability to stay with one focus in daily tasks.

Real-World Example: The Focused Student

Ethan, a law student, struggled with distraction while preparing for exams. He tried studying for hours but constantly shifted between texts, notes, and online browsing. After adopting single-tasking, he dedicated 45-minute blocks to one subject, with breaks between. He also practiced mindfulness to quiet his internal noise. Within a month, his concentration improved, and his exam scores reflected the change. He discovered that clarity was less about effort and more about focus.

The Deeper Reward: Presence

Beyond productivity, single-tasking cultivates presence. It allows you to fully experience life as it unfolds. Eating without screens restores the richness of flavor. Listening without distraction deepens connection in relationships. Walking without a phone opens space for observation and creativity.

Presence is the essence of clarity. When attention is not fractured, life feels fuller, calmer, and more meaningful.

Takeaway: Depth in a Noisy World

In a world that celebrates multitasking and constant noise, single-task focus is revolutionary. It is the practice of reclaiming attention from distraction and directing it toward what matters. The benefits extend beyond productivity—they touch creativity, emotional well-being, and presence itself.

Building single-task focus requires environment design, boundaries, rituals, and internal training. But the reward is profound: a mind no longer scattered but aligned, capable of depth in a noisy world.

Entering Flow State with Intention

There are moments in life when everything seems to align: work feels effortless, time disappears, and performance peaks. Writers describe words pouring out naturally. Athletes describe being "in the zone." Musicians describe losing themselves in rhythm. Psychologists call this phenomenon **flow state**—a condition of deep immersion and optimal experience.

Flow is not accidental; it is a state that can be cultivated. Yet many people experience it only sporadically, stumbling into it by chance. By understanding the psychology of flow and practicing the conditions that foster it, we can learn to enter flow state with intention. Doing so transforms productivity, creativity, and mental freedom.

What Is Flow State?

The term "flow" was introduced by psychologist Mihaly Csikszentmihalyi, who studied the experiences of artists, athletes, and professionals who reported being completely absorbed in their work. Flow is characterized by:

- Complete concentration on the task at hand
- A merging of action and awareness
- A sense of control without conscious effort
- Distorted perception of time (either speeding up or slowing down)
- Intrinsic reward—the activity feels fulfilling in itself

In flow, the mind and body operate in harmony. Effort feels natural, distractions fade, and performance rises beyond ordinary levels.

The Neuroscience of Flow

Flow state is associated with a unique neurological pattern called **transient hypofrontality**—a temporary downregulation of the prefrontal cortex. This reduces self-consciousness and inner chatter, allowing action to unfold smoothly. Simultaneously, the brain releases dopamine, norepinephrine, and endorphins, enhancing focus, motivation, and enjoyment.

In addition, alpha and theta brain waves—associated with creativity and relaxation—dominate during flow. This explains why flow often feels both intensely focused and strangely calm.

The Conditions of Flow

Csikszentmihalyi identified several key conditions necessary for flow:

1. **Clear Goals**
   The mind focuses best when the objective is specific. Ambiguity scatters attention; clarity directs it.
2. **Immediate Feedback**
   Flow requires real-time information about progress. This feedback loop keeps the brain engaged and adaptive.
3. **Balance Between Challenge and Skill**
   Flow emerges at the edge of ability—tasks that are too easy lead to boredom, while tasks that are too hard create anxiety. Flow thrives when challenge slightly exceeds skill, stretching capacity.
4. **Deep Focus**
   Distraction is the enemy of flow. Sustained attention allows immersion.

Everyday Examples of Flow

- A coder working through a complex problem, losing track of hours as solutions unfold
- A basketball player moving seamlessly with the rhythm of the game
- A chef preparing a meal with such concentration that every chop and stir feels precise and rhythmic
- A reader so absorbed in a novel that the world around them disappears

Flow is not limited to extraordinary performers—it is accessible in daily life, from work to hobbies to personal growth.

The Barriers to Flow

While flow is natural, modern environments create barriers:

- **Distractions:** Notifications, interruptions, and noise pull attention away before immersion can begin.
- **Multitasking:** Dividing attention prevents the deep focus required for flow.

- **Fear of Failure:** Self-consciousness disrupts the merging of action and awareness.
- **Lack of Clarity:** Unclear goals or vague tasks scatter focus.

Recognizing these barriers is the first step to overcoming them.

Real-World Case Study: The Athlete's Zone

Jordan, a competitive swimmer, often struggled with performance anxiety. During meets, his mind filled with self-criticism: *What if I lose? What if I disappoint my coach?* These thoughts disrupted his rhythm. With training, Jordan learned to focus solely on technique and rhythm—one stroke at a time. By setting clear goals and silencing inner chatter, he began entering flow during races. His performance improved, not because he tried harder, but because he let go of self-consciousness.

Entering Flow with Intention

Flow may feel spontaneous, but it can be cultivated deliberately. Here are practices to build conditions for flow:

1. Define Clear Goals
Before beginning a task, specify exactly what you want to accomplish. Instead of "write today," set: "draft 500 words of chapter one." Clarity directs attention.

2. Match Challenge to Skill
Identify your current skill level and choose tasks that stretch you just beyond it. If too easy, raise the challenge. If too hard, break it into smaller steps.

3. Eliminate Distractions
Silence notifications, close unnecessary tabs, and create a focused environment. Flow cannot coexist with interruptions.

4. Use Rituals to Begin
Start tasks with a consistent ritual—a breathing exercise, a specific playlist, or a set workspace. Rituals train the brain to enter focus mode.

5. Work in Time Blocks
Flow often takes 15–20 minutes to emerge. Dedicate at least 60–90 minutes to deep work sessions. Avoid frequent task-switching.

6. Embrace Feedback Loops
Seek immediate feedback where possible. For example, writers re-read sentences, athletes track performance, and gamers see scores instantly. Feedback sustains engagement.

7. Train Self-Awareness
Notice when boredom or anxiety pulls you out of flow. Adjust challenge or skill level accordingly.

Flow in Work

In professional life, flow transforms productivity. Engineers designing solutions, teachers deeply engaged with students, or entrepreneurs solving problems can all enter flow. Companies that encourage deep work over constant multitasking create cultures where innovation thrives.

Flow in Creativity

Artists often describe flow as their natural state of creation. Painters immersed in color, musicians in melody, or writers in narrative tap into a space where imagination feels limitless. Creativity blossoms when the conscious mind quiets and deeper processes take over.

Flow in Everyday Life

Flow is not confined to work or art. Cooking a meal with presence, gardening with care, or even cleaning mindfully can create flow. Any task that balances challenge and skill, with focus and clarity, holds potential for flow.

The Long-Term Benefits of Flow

Regularly entering flow enhances mental health and performance:

- **Happiness and Fulfillment:** Flow is intrinsically rewarding. People who experience more flow report higher life satisfaction.
- **Skill Development:** Flow accelerates learning because it stretches ability at the edge of comfort.
- **Resilience:** Flow provides a refuge from stress, creating states of calm immersion that counterbalance daily pressures.
- **Identity Growth:** Flow reinforces a sense of competence and agency, strengthening confidence.

Real-World Example: The Writer's Discipline

Leah, an aspiring novelist, struggled with procrastination. Writing felt overwhelming, and she rarely entered flow. After studying flow principles, she set small, clear goals (500 words per session), eliminated distractions, and began each session with a ritual— lighting a candle and playing soft music. Over time, she began slipping into flow regularly. Writing became enjoyable, even addictive. What once felt like a struggle became a source of joy.

The Deeper Lesson: Flow as a Way of Being

Flow is not just a performance tool—it is a way of living. It teaches us to engage deeply, to find joy in the process, and to merge fully with the present moment. In a distracted world, flow offers not only productivity but also peace.

Takeaway: Designing Life for Flow

Flow is not luck. It is the natural state of a mind fully engaged, free from distraction, aligned with purpose. By setting clear goals, balancing challenge and skill, eliminating interruptions, and creating rituals, we can enter flow intentionally.

In flow, the mind is no longer fragmented. Clarity arises, performance peaks, and life feels alive. To live with freedom is not to avoid effort—it is to enter effort so fully that it becomes effortless. Flow is that path.

Energy Leaks: Hidden Habits Draining Your Mind

Mental energy is one of the most precious resources we possess. Unlike time, which is fixed, mental energy fluctuates depending on how we live, think, and act. Some days feel sharp, creative, and focused, while others feel sluggish and foggy, even if we slept and ate well. The difference often lies in energy leaks—small, hidden habits that steadily drain mental clarity without our awareness.

These leaks are rarely dramatic. They do not announce themselves as crises but creep silently into daily life. Left unchecked, they leave the mind scattered, exhausted, and reactive. By identifying and sealing these leaks, we reclaim the energy needed for focus, flow, and freedom.

Why Energy Management Matters More Than Time Management

Most people focus on managing time: calendars, schedules, and productivity hacks. While useful, time management overlooks a key truth: two hours of high energy are more valuable than six hours of fatigue. Mental energy, not time, determines the quality of work, decision-making, and creativity.

For example, an exhausted person may spend three hours completing a task that a focused mind could finish in 45 minutes. The difference is not time but energy. When hidden leaks drain energy, no amount of time management can compensate.

The Science of Mental Energy

Mental energy is not mystical—it has biological and psychological foundations.

- **Glucose and Oxygen:** The brain consumes about 20% of the body's energy. Clear thinking requires steady fuel.
- **Neurotransmitters:** Chemicals like dopamine, serotonin, and acetylcholine regulate focus and motivation.
- **Cognitive Load:** The more information the brain juggles, the more energy it consumes. Unnecessary tasks, clutter, or decisions deplete reserves.
- **Emotional Regulation:** Stress, worry, and unresolved emotions consume energy, even when no physical action occurs.

This explains why energy leaks often go unnoticed: they drain resources silently in the background.

Hidden Habit 1: Decision Overload

Every choice consumes willpower and energy. Psychologists call this **decision fatigue.** From trivial choices like what to wear to major decisions at work, each choice depletes mental reserves. When small, unnecessary decisions pile up, clarity suffers.

Practical Fix: Simplify decisions by creating routines. Steve Jobs famously wore the same style of clothing daily to conserve decision energy. You don't need to be extreme, but creating habits around meals, outfits, or daily schedules reduces unnecessary choices, preserving energy for what matters.

Hidden Habit 2: Constant Digital Checking

Smartphones and computers encourage constant checking—emails, notifications, social media. Each check, even for seconds, fragments attention. The brain requires energy to switch tasks, and micro-switches throughout the day accumulate into fatigue.

Practical Fix: Create designated "check windows" instead of constant monitoring. For example, check email three times a day instead of 30. Turn off non-essential notifications. Place the phone out of sight during deep work.

Hidden Habit 3: Unfinished Tasks

Psychologists call this the **Zeigarnik effect**—unfinished tasks occupy mental space, draining energy even when not actively pursued. A long, unfinished to-do list creates background tension that saps clarity.

Practical Fix: Use the "two-minute rule"—if a task takes less than two minutes, do it immediately. For larger tasks, break them into clear steps and schedule them. The act of planning reduces the brain's need to hold onto them.

Hidden Habit 4: Negative Self-Talk

Internal dialogue consumes energy. Self-criticism, worry, or rumination drains mental bandwidth, leaving less for focus. Even subtle negative thoughts accumulate into fatigue.

Practical Fix: Practice cognitive reframing. When a negative thought arises—"I can't do this"—reframe to: "This is challenging, but I can take one step." Reframing shifts energy from depletion to empowerment.

Hidden Habit 5: Cluttered Environment

Physical clutter creates cognitive clutter. Studies show that messy environments increase cortisol and reduce the brain's ability to focus. Each object in view is processed subconsciously, creating background noise.

Practical Fix: Dedicate a few minutes daily to tidying. Keep workspaces clear and organized. A minimalist environment conserves attention for meaningful tasks.

Hidden Habit 6: Energy-Draining Relationships

Interactions with others either energize or deplete. Toxic relationships, constant complainers, or manipulative influences drain emotional energy, even if time spent is brief.

Practical Fix: Set boundaries with draining individuals. Limit exposure where possible and prioritize relationships that uplift and support.

Hidden Habit 7: Poor Transitions Between Tasks

Jumping abruptly from one task to another without closure creates lingering cognitive residue. This residue carries into the next task, reducing focus.

Practical Fix: Create transition rituals. Take three deep breaths, stretch, or write a closing note before shifting tasks. This signals the brain to release one task and fully engage in the next.

Hidden Habit 8: Overcommitment

Saying yes too often spreads energy thin. Each obligation consumes mental space, even if not urgent. Overcommitment leads to shallow engagement in many tasks rather than deep engagement in a few.

Practical Fix: Practice saying no with clarity. Evaluate commitments against priorities. Ask: "Does this align with my values and goals?"

Real-World Case Study: The Overwhelmed Professional

Lena, a financial analyst, often felt exhausted despite working reasonable hours. She discovered her energy leaks: checking email 50 times a day, maintaining cluttered workspaces, and agreeing to too many side projects. By consolidating email checks, decluttering her desk, and declining non-essential commitments, Lena regained energy. Her productivity increased not because she worked more hours but because she stopped leaking energy.

The Role of Rest in Energy Management

Sealing leaks is vital, but replenishing energy is equally important. Rest is not wasted time—it is a requirement for clarity. Sleep restores memory, creativity, and emotional regulation. Breaks during the day prevent burnout. Without rest, even sealed leaks cannot sustain energy.

Deep Practices for Energy Renewal

1. **Sleep Hygiene**: Consistent sleep schedules, dark rooms, and reduced evening screen time restore energy overnight.
2. **Mindful Breaks**: Short pauses for breathing or stretching reset the nervous system.
3. **Nature Exposure**: Time outdoors reduces stress and restores attention.
4. **Movement**: Exercise increases blood flow and neurotransmitters, renewing energy.

Energy Leaks and Identity

Often, people cling to energy-draining habits because they are tied to identity. For example, someone may believe "I must always be available" and therefore check emails constantly. Recognizing that freedom requires shifting identity—seeing oneself as someone who protects energy—creates lasting change.

The Bigger Picture: Energy as a Currency

Mental energy is like money: it can be invested wisely, wasted carelessly, or drained by hidden expenses. Without awareness, leaks quietly bankrupt clarity. With awareness, energy becomes a currency for focus, creativity, and joy.

Takeaway: Protecting the Invisible Resource

The greatest drain on clarity is not always visible effort but hidden leaks. Decision fatigue, digital checking, unfinished tasks, negative self-talk, clutter, draining relationships, poor transitions, and overcommitment all siphon mental energy.

By sealing these leaks and prioritizing renewal, we reclaim energy for what truly matters. Mental freedom is not about doing more—it is about directing energy intentionally, conserving it where it is wasted, and investing it where it creates growth.

When you protect energy, clarity emerges naturally. Your mind becomes sharper, calmer, and more resilient—not by adding more effort but by eliminating silent drains.

Daily Micro-Rituals to Recharge Attention

Attention is the foundation of clarity. It determines not only what we focus on but also how we experience life. Yet attention is fragile. In the modern world, it is constantly pulled by notifications, responsibilities, and distractions. Long hours of work, endless decisions, and hidden energy leaks steadily deplete it. When attention is drained, even simple tasks feel overwhelming, relationships lose depth, and creativity diminishes.

The good news is that attention can be recharged. Just as physical energy is renewed through food and sleep, mental attention can be restored through intentional practices. These practices need not be lengthy or complicated. In fact, the most effective ones are often **micro-rituals**—short, simple activities embedded into daily routines that reset the mind and restore focus.

Micro-rituals are powerful because they are consistent, easy to repeat, and aligned with natural rhythms. They create moments of pause, reflection, and renewal, preventing the buildup of mental fatigue. By weaving them into daily life, we transform attention from something fragile into something resilient.

Why Micro-Rituals Work

Micro-rituals leverage several psychological and physiological mechanisms:

- **Interrupting Automaticity:** They break the autopilot of busyness, allowing conscious reset.
- **Engaging the Parasympathetic Nervous System:** Many rituals calm the body, lowering cortisol and stress.
- **Anchoring Attention:** Rituals provide cues that bring the mind back to the present moment.
- **Creating Predictability:** Repeated rituals reduce decision fatigue by establishing consistent habits.

Unlike large, occasional practices (like vacations), micro-rituals work daily. They don't require special conditions; they adapt to ordinary life.

The Myth of Endless Focus

One reason people struggle with attention is the belief that it should last endlessly. In reality, research shows the brain's capacity for deep focus typically lasts 60–90 minutes before fatigue sets in. Micro-rituals provide recovery periods that allow focus to be sustained throughout the day. Without them, attention depletes quickly, leading to distraction and procrastination.

Ritual 1: The Morning Anchor

The way we begin the day sets the tone for attention. Many people start by checking phones, flooding the brain with information before it is ready. This creates reactive, fragmented attention from the outset.

A morning anchor ritual focuses the mind before external demands intrude. Examples include:

- Five minutes of deep breathing or meditation
- Journaling intentions for the day
- Stretching while visualizing focus
- Reading a few pages of inspiring material

Even five minutes creates an intentional start that anchors attention.

Ritual 2: The Breathing Reset

Breath is the fastest tool for recharging attention. Shallow, rapid breathing signals stress, while slow, deep breathing restores calm.

One effective technique is **box breathing:** inhale for four counts, hold for four, exhale for four, hold for four. Repeat for a few cycles.

This can be practiced between tasks, during transitions, or whenever distraction arises. It requires no equipment and works in minutes.

Ritual 3: Micro-Movement Breaks

The brain thrives on oxygen and blood flow. Long periods of sitting reduce circulation, leading to fatigue and fog. Short bursts of movement restore energy and focus.

Examples include:

- Standing to stretch every hour
- Walking for five minutes between tasks
- Doing a set of push-ups, squats, or yoga poses

These breaks are not about fitness; they are about recharging the brain through movement.

Ritual 4: Single-Task Meals

Eating while scrolling, working, or watching screens fragments attention. Single-task eating transforms meals into rituals of presence and renewal.

Practice:

- Set aside devices during meals
- Notice flavors, textures, and sensations
- Eat slowly, focusing only on the experience

This not only improves digestion but also re-centers attention before returning to work.

Ritual 5: Digital Pauses

Screens dominate attention. Continuous scrolling, notifications, and digital overload drain focus. Scheduled digital pauses create micro-moments of renewal.

Practice:

- Set three specific times to check messages instead of constant monitoring
- Use app timers to limit social media use
- Designate tech-free spaces (like the dining table or bedroom)

These pauses prevent digital leakage and preserve attention for meaningful tasks.

Ritual 6: The Gratitude Pause

Gratitude shifts the mind from scarcity to abundance. This positive focus recharges attention by reducing stress and broadening perspective.

Practice:

- At midday or evening, write down three things you are grateful for
- Pause for 30 seconds with each, feeling the emotion fully

This simple ritual counters negativity bias, training attention toward appreciation rather than complaint.

Ritual 7: The Evening Reflection

The day often ends with lingering mental clutter—unfinished tasks, worries, or replayed conversations. Evening reflection clears the mental desk, allowing restful sleep and a fresh start tomorrow.

Practice:

- Spend five minutes writing: "What went well today? What can I improve? What do I release before sleep?"
- Close with one intention for tomorrow

This ritual prevents rumination at night and sets up clarity for the morning.

Ritual 8: The Transition Cue

Many people struggle to shift from work to home or from one role to another. Without clear transitions, attention remains scattered. Transition rituals signal closure and reset.

Examples include:

- Writing a "done list" at the end of work
- Changing clothes immediately upon returning home
- Listening to specific music during commutes

These cues help the brain let go of one context and fully engage in the next.

Ritual 9: Nature Micro-Doses

Exposure to nature restores attention more effectively than artificial environments. Even small doses create measurable benefits.

Practice:

- Spend five minutes outdoors observing the sky, plants, or sounds
- Place a plant near your desk and pause to notice it during breaks
- Walk barefoot on grass or soil to reconnect physically

Nature engages the brain's restorative mode, allowing focus to recharge.

Ritual 10: The Mini-Meditation

Formal meditation can be daunting, but mini-meditations fit seamlessly into daily life.

Practice:

- Close your eyes and focus on three deep breaths
- Repeat a calming word or phrase silently for one minute
- Visualize light or warmth filling the body

Even one minute can reset attention when practiced consistently.

Real-World Case Study: The Teacher's Renewal

Carla, a high school teacher, often felt mentally exhausted by midday. She introduced micro-rituals: deep breathing before each class, gratitude journaling during lunch, and evening reflection. Within weeks, her energy improved. She no longer ended the day depleted. By recharging attention through small, consistent rituals, she regained clarity and presence for both work and home life.

How to Embed Micro-Rituals Into Life

The effectiveness of rituals lies in consistency, not complexity. To embed them:

- **Start Small:** Choose one ritual and practice it daily before adding others.
- **Pair With Existing Habits:** Attach rituals to current routines, like breathing before opening a laptop or gratitude before meals.
- **Use Triggers:** Set alarms or visual cues (like a sticky note) to remind you.
- **Keep Flexible:** Adapt rituals to context—standing stretches at home, short walks at the office.

Over time, these rituals become automatic, creating a rhythm of renewal throughout the day.

The Deeper Lesson: Attention as a Cycle

Attention is not static—it follows cycles of focus and recovery. Expecting constant concentration leads to burnout. Micro-rituals respect this rhythm by providing mini-recoveries, ensuring attention remains sharp and sustainable.

Just as athletes alternate between training and rest, the mind performs best when periods of deep focus are balanced with micro-renewals.

Takeaway: Small Acts, Big Freedom

Daily micro-rituals recharge attention by interrupting distraction, calming the nervous system, and restoring presence. They transform ordinary moments—meals, breaks, transitions—into opportunities for renewal.

Mental freedom is not built in grand gestures but in small, consistent acts. By practicing micro-rituals, we protect attention from depletion, reclaim clarity, and create a sustainable rhythm of focus in a noisy world.

CHAPTER 5

Breaking the Cycle of Overthinking

Why the Brain Loves to Loop Thoughts

Most people know the experience of lying awake at night replaying a conversation, worrying about the future, or rehearsing worst-case scenarios. The mind circles endlessly, offering no new insights yet refusing to stop. This is overthinking—a cycle of thought loops that drain energy and clarity.

Why does the brain do this? On the surface, looping thoughts seem irrational. They waste time, heighten anxiety, and rarely solve problems. Yet, when examined through neuroscience and psychology, overthinking makes sense. The brain loves to loop thoughts because looping feels like control, preparation, or problem-solving, even when it is not. Understanding why the brain loops thoughts is the first step to breaking free from the cycle of overthinking.

The Brain's Survival Bias

The brain's primary job is survival, not happiness. From an evolutionary perspective, vigilance kept our ancestors alive. Those who constantly scanned for threats—dangerous animals, hostile tribes, environmental risks—were more likely to survive than those who relaxed too soon.

This survival bias persists today. The brain interprets unresolved issues as potential threats. When a problem feels unsolved, the brain keeps circling it in an attempt to protect us. This explains why worries about money, relationships, or work replay endlessly. The brain treats uncertainty as danger and responds with looping thoughts.

The Illusion of Control

Another reason the brain loops is the illusion of control. Thinking about something repeatedly feels like doing something about it. Rehearsing a conflict in your head, worrying about an exam, or replaying a mistake creates the sensation of preparation. In reality, the looping often substitutes for action without producing solutions.

This illusion is powerful because it soothes anxiety temporarily. But the relief is fleeting, so the brain returns to the loop, creating a cycle.

The Role of the Default Mode Network

Neuroscience provides further explanation. When the brain is not engaged in a specific task, it activates the **default mode network (DMN)**—a set of regions associated with self-referential thought, memory, and imagination. The DMN is useful for reflection and creativity, but when overactive, it fuels rumination and worry.

An overactive DMN loops on past regrets ("Why did I say that?") or future fears ("What if this goes wrong?"). Without regulation, the DMN hijacks attention, pulling the mind away from the present.

The Reward Cycle of Rumination

Overthinking is not only about fear—it also taps into reward pathways. Each time the brain loops on a problem, it releases a small amount of dopamine, rewarding the sense of effort. This creates a reinforcement cycle: the brain learns that looping is "helpful," even when it is not.

This explains why breaking thought loops feels difficult. The brain has been conditioned to treat overthinking as useful, even as it drains clarity.

The Emotional Amplifier

Thought loops intensify emotions. A small worry becomes magnified by repeated attention. For example, a single comment from a colleague may trigger insecurity. Replaying the comment magnifies the insecurity, fueling more loops. This cycle creates emotional spirals where the thought fuels the feeling, and the feeling fuels more thoughts.

Real-World Case Study: The Overthinking Professional

Marcus, a young lawyer, often found himself stuck in thought loops after client meetings. He replayed conversations endlessly, analyzing whether he had said the "right" thing. These loops consumed hours and drained his energy. When examined, Marcus realized the loops gave him the illusion of control: if he replayed enough, he might prevent mistakes in the future. Yet the replay produced no solutions—only exhaustion. His experience illustrates how the brain mistakes looping for preparation.

Overthinking vs. Problem-Solving

It's important to distinguish overthinking from genuine problem-solving. Problem-solving involves structured steps: identifying the issue, generating solutions, evaluating options, and acting. Overthinking, by contrast, circles endlessly without resolution.

A useful question to break the cycle is: *Am I thinking about solutions or am I just replaying?* If no new insight emerges, it is overthinking, not problem-solving.

Cognitive Biases That Fuel Loops

Several psychological biases contribute to looping thoughts:

- **Negativity Bias:** The brain gives more weight to negative events than positive ones, leading to disproportionate replay of fears or mistakes.
- **Catastrophizing:** Imagining worst-case scenarios and looping on them, regardless of likelihood.
- **Perfectionism:** Believing only flawless performance is acceptable, leading to endless mental rehearsal.

- **Hindsight Bias:** Replaying past mistakes with the illusion that they should have been obvious at the time.

These biases distort perspective and keep the brain locked in loops.

The Cost of Thought Loops

Overthinking carries hidden costs:

- **Cognitive Fatigue:** Loops consume mental energy, leaving less for productive focus.
- **Sleep Disruption:** Nighttime rumination delays sleep and reduces rest quality.
- **Reduced Creativity:** Constant replay leaves little room for new ideas.
- **Emotional Strain:** Loops amplify stress, anxiety, and self-doubt.

The cost is not only personal—relationships and work also suffer when attention is trapped in loops.

Why Loops Persist

Despite their cost, loops persist because they provide short-term comfort. They give the illusion of effort, reduce uncertainty momentarily, and keep the brain engaged. But like scratching an itch, the relief is temporary. The underlying issue remains unresolved.

Breaking the Loop: Awareness as the First Step

The first step to breaking loops is awareness. Most people are unaware they are caught in overthinking until hours have passed. Simply labeling the loop—"This is a thought loop"—creates distance. Awareness interrupts automaticity and opens the possibility of choice.

Real-World Example: The Student's Exam Anxiety

Sophia, a medical student, often looped on exam fears: *What if I fail? What if I forget everything?* Her mind circled without rest. Through mindfulness training, she learned to notice the loop and label it: *This is a worry loop.* By naming it, she created enough space to shift focus to productive studying. Awareness did not erase worry instantly, but it broke the automatic cycle.

The Deeper Lesson: Loops as Unmet Needs

At a deeper level, thought loops often signal unmet needs. A loop about work may reflect a need for reassurance, clarity, or preparation. A loop about relationships may reflect a need for connection or security. Recognizing the underlying need transforms the loop from enemy to messenger. Instead of replaying endlessly, the mind can address the need directly.

Takeaway: The Brain Loops for Survival, Not Clarity

The brain loves to loop thoughts because loops feel protective—maintaining vigilance, creating the illusion of control, and offering short-term comfort. Yet loops rarely solve problems; they drain clarity and energy instead.

By recognizing why loops occur—evolutionary bias, the default mode network, dopamine reinforcement, and cognitive distortions—we gain power to interrupt them. Awareness, reframing, and addressing unmet needs break the cycle.

Freedom begins with understanding: overthinking is not a personal flaw but a brain mechanism gone unchecked. When we see this clearly, we stop blaming ourselves and start reclaiming attention.

Recognizing Decision Fatigue

Every day, human beings make thousands of decisions, from the trivial—what to eat for breakfast, what shirt to wear—to the significant—how to handle a conflict, whether to take a new job, or how to respond in a crisis. While it may feel like each choice is independent, research shows that decision-making draws from a limited pool of mental energy. As this pool is depleted, the quality of decisions declines. This phenomenon is known as **decision fatigue.**

Decision fatigue explains why people make poor choices late in the day, why willpower weakens after repeated decisions, and why even simple choices can feel overwhelming when we are mentally drained. Recognizing decision fatigue is essential for breaking cycles of overthinking, because many thought loops are fueled by exhausted decision-making systems. By understanding how decision fatigue works and learning to manage it, we protect clarity and preserve energy for what matters most.

The Science Behind Decision Fatigue

The brain consumes vast amounts of energy to make decisions. Each choice activates the prefrontal cortex, the region responsible for weighing options, predicting consequences, and exercising self-control. The more decisions made, the more these circuits tire.

Psychologists Roy Baumeister and Kathleen Vohs pioneered research on **ego depletion**—the idea that self-control and decision-making rely on a finite reservoir of mental energy. Their experiments showed that after making many choices, people are more likely to act impulsively, avoid decisions altogether, or default to the easiest option.

Later studies refined this view, showing that decision fatigue is less about absolute depletion and more about the brain's shifting allocation of energy. Regardless of mechanism, the outcome is the same: repeated decisions erode clarity and self-control.

Signs of Decision Fatigue

Recognizing decision fatigue requires noticing its subtle symptoms. Common signs include:

- **Procrastination:** Delaying choices, even small ones.
- **Impulsivity:** Opting for the easiest or most tempting option without reflection.
- **Avoidance:** Ignoring decisions altogether.
- **Irritability:** Feeling impatient or overwhelmed by requests.
- **Mental Fog:** Struggling to weigh options or think clearly.

These symptoms often arise later in the day or after periods of heavy decision-making.

Real-World Case Study: The Parole Board

One striking example comes from a study of parole hearings in Israel. Researchers found that judges were far more likely to grant parole early in the day or after breaks, while approvals dropped dramatically later in sessions. The explanation was not bias against prisoners but decision fatigue—after repeated choices, judges defaulted to the safest option: denial.

This illustrates how decision fatigue can shape high-stakes outcomes without awareness.

Everyday Examples of Decision Fatigue

- A student studies effectively in the morning but struggles to choose answers on practice tests at night.
- A shopper resists unhealthy snacks early in the day but caves to cravings in the evening.
- A parent manages conflicts patiently in the morning but loses temper easily by bedtime.

These patterns reflect the hidden influence of decision fatigue across daily life.

Why Modern Life Intensifies Decision Fatigue

In earlier times, daily life involved fewer discretionary choices. Today, the sheer volume of options intensifies fatigue. From dozens of toothpaste brands to hundreds of streaming options, the abundance of choice creates constant micro-decisions. Add to this emails, messages, and digital notifications, and the brain faces decision overload before the day even begins.

The Link Between Overthinking and Decision Fatigue

Overthinking and decision fatigue reinforce each other. When fatigued, the brain struggles to make decisions, leading to looping thoughts: *Should I do this or that? What if I choose wrong?* The loop prolongs decision-making, which drains energy further, creating a vicious cycle.

Breaking free requires not only managing overthinking but also reducing unnecessary decisions that fuel fatigue.

Practical Strategies to Reduce Decision Fatigue

1. Automate Routine Choices
Simplify recurring decisions by creating habits or systems. Examples:

- Meal prepping for the week
- Wearing a simplified wardrobe
- Setting fixed morning or evening routines

Automation reduces trivial choices, conserving energy for meaningful decisions.

2. Prioritize Important Decisions Early
Schedule critical decisions when energy is highest, often in the morning. Avoid leaving significant choices for late in the day.

3. Limit Options
More options may seem liberating but increase cognitive load. Narrow choices intentionally—for example, select from three restaurants instead of 20.

4. Use Decision Frameworks
Apply simple rules for recurring decisions:

- "If it takes less than two minutes, do it immediately."
- "If it doesn't align with goals, decline."

Frameworks reduce the need for deliberation.

5. Take Recovery Breaks
Short breaks, naps, or walks restore energy and improve subsequent decision-making. The brain is not a machine; it requires recovery.

6. Delegate or Share Decisions
Not all choices require personal attention. Delegate routine decisions to others or share responsibility when appropriate.

7. Recognize When to Stop
Sometimes the best decision is to pause. If clarity is gone, step back and return later with renewed energy.

Real-World Example: The CEO's Routine

Many CEOs minimize decision fatigue by simplifying daily routines. Barack Obama and Mark Zuckerberg, for example, deliberately wore similar outfits daily to avoid trivial decisions. By conserving energy on small choices, they preserved clarity for significant leadership decisions.

The Role of Sleep and Nutrition

Decision fatigue is amplified by poor sleep and diet. Sleep restores prefrontal cortex function, while glucose provides fuel for decision-making. Sleep deprivation or erratic blood sugar levels make the brain more vulnerable to fatigue. Consistent rest and balanced nutrition support sustained clarity.

Emotional Regulation and Decision Fatigue

Emotions play a key role in decisions. When emotionally drained, people are more likely to make reactive or short-sighted choices. This explains why conflicts escalate late in the day—decision fatigue reduces patience and emotional regulation. Managing emotions through mindfulness, breathing, or breaks prevents fatigue from spiraling into poor judgment.

The Deeper Lesson: Not Every Decision Deserves Equal Energy

One of the most liberating insights about decision fatigue is realizing that not all choices deserve equal weight. Many people waste mental energy deliberating over trivial matters while neglecting what truly matters. Recognizing this imbalance helps direct energy toward high-impact decisions.

Ask: *Does this choice significantly affect my values, goals, or well-being?* If not, simplify or automate. If yes, schedule it for peak energy times.

Takeaway: Protecting Clarity by Protecting Energy

Decision fatigue is not weakness—it is biology. The brain's decision-making systems tire with use, leading to procrastination, impulsivity, or avoidance. In a world overflowing with choices, managing this fatigue is essential for clarity.

By automating routines, prioritizing early, limiting options, using frameworks, taking breaks, and maintaining rest and nutrition, we reduce fatigue and preserve energy for what matters most.

Mental freedom is not about making perfect choices in every moment—it is about protecting the mind's energy so it can make the right choices when they matter most. Recognizing decision fatigue allows us to live with intention rather than exhaustion.

Tools for Rapid Decision-Making

Overthinking thrives in the space between options. When faced with choices, the brain often stalls, circling endlessly in search of the "perfect" decision. While reflection is valuable, excessive deliberation drains energy, fuels anxiety, and prevents progress. One of the most powerful ways to break the cycle of overthinking is to develop tools for rapid decision-making—methods that allow choices to be made efficiently without being paralyzed by analysis.

Rapid decision-making does not mean reckless impulsivity. It means creating frameworks, habits, and strategies that cut through unnecessary loops and allow for clear, timely choices. In a world of overwhelming options, mastering this skill is essential for mental clarity and freedom.

Why the Brain Struggles with Decisions

Before exploring tools, it is helpful to understand why decisions feel so difficult.

1. **Fear of Regret**
   Many people hesitate because they fear choosing "wrong." The brain magnifies potential losses more than potential gains—a phenomenon called **loss aversion.** This bias makes even small choices feel weighty.

2. **Perfectionism**
   The belief that there is one perfect choice keeps the mind circling indefinitely. In reality, most decisions have multiple workable outcomes.
3. **Information Overload**
   The modern world bombards us with data. More options may appear beneficial but often overwhelm the brain, leading to decision paralysis.
4. **Emotional Interference**
   Strong emotions—fear, guilt, excitement—cloud rational evaluation, creating hesitation or impulsivity.

Recognizing these forces allows us to see indecision not as weakness but as a predictable brain response. Tools for rapid decision-making provide structure to bypass these traps.

The 80/20 Rule for Decisions

The **Pareto Principle**, or 80/20 rule, states that 80% of results often come from 20% of inputs. Applied to decision-making, this means most outcomes are shaped by a few key choices, while many smaller ones have minimal impact.

When facing a decision, ask: *Is this a high-impact decision or a low-impact one?* If low-impact, decide quickly and move on. Reserve deep analysis for high-impact decisions. This prevents wasted energy on trivial matters.

The Two-Minute Rule

If a decision takes less than two minutes to make, decide immediately. This rule prevents small choices—like what email to send or what item to order—from snowballing into loops. Rapid resolution of small decisions preserves energy for larger ones.

The 70% Rule

Former U.S. Secretary of State Colin Powell advised making decisions when you have about 70% of the information you wish you had. Waiting for 100% certainty often leads to paralysis, while acting with less than 70% risks recklessness. The 70% rule balances speed with prudence, allowing timely action without perfectionism.

Pre-Commitment and Defaults

Many decisions can be simplified through pre-commitment—choosing in advance to reduce daily deliberation. Examples include:

- Pre-planned weekly meals
- Automatic savings transfers
- Fixed workout schedules

Defaults conserve energy. When healthy choices are automated, the brain is freed from constant micro-decisions.

The "If-Then" Framework

Creating conditional rules speeds up decision-making. Examples:

- "If it costs under $20 and saves me time, I buy it."
- "If the meeting has no clear agenda, I decline."
- "If I'm stuck between two good options, I choose the one that excites me more."

These frameworks bypass looping by outsourcing decisions to pre-set rules.

Time-Limited Decisions

Indecision thrives in unlimited time. Setting deadlines forces resolution. For small decisions, give yourself minutes. For medium ones, hours or a day. For large ones, a clear timeline prevents endless circling. The key is to match decision size with decision time.

The Five-by-Five Rule

Ask: *Will this decision matter in five weeks, five months, or five years?* If not, decide quickly and release overthinking. This reframes perspective, reducing the tendency to inflate minor choices.

Gut Check vs. Head Check

Research shows intuition often draws on subconscious pattern recognition. For familiar domains, gut instinct can be highly reliable. For unfamiliar domains, rational analysis is better. Asking: *Is this familiar or new?* guides whether to trust instinct or analysis, preventing wasted loops.

The One-Move Forward Principle

Instead of seeking the perfect end decision, focus on the next move forward. Ask: *What is the smallest step that moves me closer to clarity?* This reduces overwhelm and breaks large choices into manageable actions.

Real-World Case Study: The Entrepreneur's Choice

Nina, an entrepreneur, faced paralysis choosing a marketing strategy. She kept analyzing data, fearing the "wrong" choice. Applying the 70% rule, she decided to move forward once she had enough data for reasonable confidence. She committed to testing the strategy for three months, knowing adjustments could follow. The decision freed her from weeks of looping and allowed progress.

Tools for Group Decisions

Group settings often magnify overthinking. To streamline collective choices:

- Use **clear criteria** agreed upon in advance.
- Limit brainstorming to a set number of options.
- Employ **majority vote** for smaller decisions.
- Assign a final decision-maker for accountability.

These structures prevent endless debate and wasted energy.

The Role of Values in Decision-Making

Decisions align more easily when guided by values. Many loops occur because people focus on external outcomes rather than internal alignment. Asking: *Which option best aligns with my values?* cuts through noise. Even if outcomes are uncertain, alignment creates peace.

Rapid Recovery From "Wrong" Decisions

Fear of mistakes fuels overthinking. Yet mistakes are inevitable. The key is not avoiding them but recovering quickly. Adopting a growth mindset—seeing mistakes as feedback—reduces the weight of each choice.

Ask: *If this turns out wrong, can I adjust? What will I learn?* With recovery plans, decisions feel less final, reducing paralysis.

Tools for Emotional Decisions

When emotions cloud clarity, try:

- **Pause and Breathe:** Allow cortisol to subside before deciding.
- **Write Options Down:** Externalizing reduces emotional bias.

- **Sleep On It:** For big decisions, rest restores rational perspective.

Emotion-regulation tools prevent impulsivity without slowing decisions unnecessarily.

Real-World Example: The Traveler's Choice

James, planning a trip, spent weeks agonizing over which city to visit. Each option seemed imperfect. Finally, he applied the five-by-five rule: in five years, the specific city would not matter; the memories would. He chose quickly and enjoyed the trip. The decision became meaningful not because of the city but because of the choice to stop looping.

The Deeper Lesson: Progress Over Perfection

Rapid decision-making is not about perfect choices—it is about momentum. Overthinking keeps life on pause, waiting for certainty that never comes. Rapid decision tools prioritize progress, knowing that most choices are adjustable. Clarity emerges not before action but through action.

Takeaway: Freedom Through Timely Choices

The brain loves to loop because it seeks certainty and control. But endless loops drain energy and prevent progress. Tools for rapid decision-making—like the 80/20 rule, the two-minute rule, the 70% rule, pre-commitments, time limits, value alignment, and recovery strategies—provide structure to bypass paralysis.

Mental freedom comes not from perfect choices but from timely ones. By acting with clarity rather than looping endlessly, we reclaim energy, momentum, and peace. Decisions no longer imprison the mind—they become steps on the path of growth.

Cognitive Reframing: Shifting Perspectives Instantly

One of the greatest traps of overthinking is the rigidity of perspective. When caught in loops, the mind fixates on one interpretation of events—often negative or exaggerated—and replays it endlessly. A disagreement becomes a disaster. A mistake becomes a permanent flaw. A challenge becomes insurmountable. In these moments, the problem is not reality itself but the lens through which reality is viewed.

Cognitive reframing is the art of shifting that lens. It is a psychological strategy that helps individuals reinterpret situations, thoughts, and emotions in ways that reduce stress and open possibilities. Reframing does not deny reality; it transforms the meaning we assign to it. By learning to reframe, we can break free from thought loops and restore clarity instantly.

The Psychology of Reframing

Cognitive reframing is rooted in **cognitive-behavioral therapy (CBT)**, one of the most evidence-based approaches in psychology. CBT teaches that our thoughts, emotions, and behaviors are interconnected. Change the thought, and the emotion and behavior follow.

For example, the thought *"I failed this exam, so I am a failure"* leads to despair. Reframing it as *"I failed this exam, which shows me where to improve"* leads to motivation. The situation is the same; the meaning is different.

The human brain naturally frames experiences. But without awareness, these frames are often distorted by biases, fears, or past wounds. Reframing is the conscious act of adjusting the frame to create a healthier perspective.

Why Reframing Breaks Thought Loops

Thought loops persist because the brain is stuck in one interpretation. Reframing interrupts the cycle by introducing a new interpretation, loosening the grip of the loop.

Consider someone looping on a breakup: *"I will never find love again."* This loop amplifies pain. Reframing to *"This breakup is painful, but it frees me to find a healthier relationship"* shifts perspective, reducing the need for endless replay.

Reframing breaks loops by offering alternative meanings, reducing emotional intensity, and opening paths to action.

The Neuroscience of Perspective

Neuroscience shows that reframing changes brain activity. Studies using functional MRI reveal that reframing negative events reduces activity in the amygdala (the brain's fear center) and increases activity in the prefrontal cortex (the center for reasoning and regulation). In essence, reframing shifts the brain from emotional reactivity to rational clarity.

This explains why reframing often feels like relief: it literally calms the nervous system.

Common Cognitive Distortions That Fuel Loops

Reframing is especially powerful when applied to cognitive distortions—habitual errors in thinking that fuel overthinking. Common distortions include:

- **Catastrophizing:** Imagining the worst-case scenario.
- **Black-and-White Thinking:** Seeing things as all good or all bad.
- **Mind Reading:** Assuming others think negatively about you without evidence.

- **Personalization:** Believing you are the cause of everything that goes wrong.
- **Overgeneralization:** Drawing broad conclusions from single events.

By identifying and reframing these distortions, we can stop them from trapping us in cycles.

Practical Reframing Techniques

1. The "What Else Could This Mean?" Question
When stuck in one interpretation, ask: *What else could this mean?* For example:

- Thought: "She didn't reply to my message, she must be upset with me."
- Reframe: "She might just be busy."

2. The Helicopter View
Zoom out mentally. Imagine observing the situation from a distance, as if watching someone else's life. How would you view it with perspective? This reduces emotional intensity and reveals new angles.

3. Reframe Failure as Feedback
Instead of seeing mistakes as final, view them as data for growth. Each misstep becomes information, not identity.

4. Temporal Reframing
Ask: *Will this matter in one week? One year? Five years?* This reduces the weight of small events.

5. Gratitude Reframing
Ask: *What is one thing I can be grateful for in this situation?* Gratitude shifts attention from scarcity to abundance, reframing even challenges as opportunities.

6. Humor as a Reframe

Humor lightens perspective. Finding something absurd or ironic in a situation reduces its power to consume thought loops.

7. Reframing "Have To" into "Get To"

Shift from obligation to opportunity. *"I have to go to work"* becomes *"I get to contribute and earn."* This subtle shift changes energy.

Real-World Case Study: The Job Rejection

A young professional, Daniel, was devastated after being rejected from a dream job. His thought loop was: *"This proves I'm not good enough."* A mentor helped him reframe: *"This shows me where I need to grow, and it frees me to find an even better fit."* Months later, he secured a job more aligned with his skills. The reframing did not change the rejection but changed how he engaged with it.

The Role of Self-Talk

Reframing often begins with self-talk. Our inner dialogue shapes our interpretation of events. By consciously shifting language, we shift frames. For instance, instead of *"This is impossible"*, saying *"This is challenging, but possible step by step"* changes both emotion and action.

Reframing in Relationships

Reframing is especially powerful in relationships. A partner's criticism can be reframed as: *"They are frustrated, but they also care about this issue."* A child's tantrum can be reframed as: *"They are overwhelmed, not ungrateful."* This shift reduces conflict and fosters empathy.

Real-World Example: The Athlete's Perspective

Emma, a runner, injured her knee before a major race. Her initial thought loop: *"All my training was wasted."* With reframing, she shifted: *"This is an opportunity to develop strength in other areas and return stronger."* The injury remained, but her perspective restored motivation and reduced despair.

How to Practice Reframing Daily

1. **Catch the Loop**: Notice when a thought repeats without progress.
2. **Label the Distortion**: Identify if it's catastrophizing, personalization, etc.
3. **Ask a Reframing Question**: "What else could this mean? How will this look in a year? What's the opportunity here?"
4. **Adopt New Language**: Use empowering words consciously.
5. **Repeat**: Reframing is a skill that strengthens with practice.

The Deeper Lesson: Freedom Lies in Perspective

Events themselves are rarely the sole source of suffering—it is the meaning we assign to them. Two people can face the same challenge, yet one feels crushed while the other grows. The difference is perspective. Reframing does not erase pain, but it prevents pain from becoming prison.

When we master reframing, we gain freedom in every situation. We can turn setbacks into lessons, stress into growth, and uncertainty into possibility. Overthinking loses power because every loop becomes an opportunity for a new frame.

Takeaway: Shift the Frame, Free the Mind

Cognitive reframing is one of the most effective tools for breaking thought loops. By shifting interpretation—through questions, perspective, humor, gratitude, or self-talk—we release the grip of negative frames.

The power lies not in changing reality but in changing the meaning we assign to it. When the frame shifts, the story shifts. And when the story shifts, the mind is free.

Journaling Techniques to Clear the Mental Fog

Overthinking thrives in silence. When thoughts remain trapped inside the mind, they circle endlessly, feeding on each other and multiplying until clarity disappears. Journaling is one of the most powerful tools for breaking this cycle. By moving thoughts from the mind onto paper, we externalize them, reducing their emotional intensity and making them easier to analyze.

Journaling does not require eloquence or perfect grammar. It is not about writing for others but writing for oneself. The purpose is clarity: clearing mental fog, identifying patterns, releasing emotions, and creating space for perspective. When practiced intentionally, journaling transforms from a simple habit into a method of mental freedom.

Why Journaling Works

The effectiveness of journaling is backed by psychology and neuroscience.

1. **Externalization of Thoughts**
   Writing shifts thoughts from the abstract world of the mind into the concrete world of paper or screen. This creates distance, allowing observation instead of entanglement.

2. **Reduced Rumination**
   Studies show expressive writing lowers rumination—the repetitive focus on distressing thoughts—by providing structured expression.
3. **Activation of the Prefrontal Cortex**
   Writing engages the rational brain, balancing emotional activation in the amygdala. This creates perspective on emotional events.
4. **Pattern Recognition**
   Journaling reveals recurring themes and distortions. Over time, patterns of overthinking become visible, making them easier to address.
5. **Emotional Release**
   Writing provides a safe outlet for unexpressed emotions, reducing the burden of suppression.

Different Approaches to Journaling

There is no single "right" way to journal. Different techniques serve different purposes. The key is choosing the method that matches your needs.

1. Freewriting (Stream of Consciousness)

Purpose: Release mental clutter and uncover hidden thoughts.

Practice:

- Set a timer for 10–20 minutes.
- Write continuously without editing or censoring.
- Let thoughts flow, even if they seem trivial or repetitive.

Benefit: Clears the mind of background noise and reveals underlying concerns.

Example: A person looping on work stress may discover, through freewriting, that their anxiety is less about deadlines and more about fear of disappointing others.

2. The Worry Dump

Purpose: Contain and release worry loops.

Practice:

- Write down every current worry, large or small.
- Next to each worry, categorize: "Within my control" or "Beyond my control."
- For controllable worries, list one action step. For uncontrollable ones, write: "Release."

Benefit: Separates solvable problems from endless loops, reducing anxiety.

3. The Gratitude Journal

Purpose: Shift focus from scarcity and fear to abundance and appreciation.

Practice:

- Each day, list three to five things you are grateful for.
- Be specific: instead of "family," write "the laugh I shared with my sister today."

Benefit: Gratitude reframes perspective, reducing the weight of negative thought loops.

4. The Cognitive Reframe Journal

Purpose: Challenge distortions and reframe negative thoughts.

Practice:

- Divide the page into two columns: Thought and Reframe.
- In the first, write looping thoughts.
- In the second, rewrite them with alternative perspectives.

Example:

- Thought: "I'm terrible at presentations."
- Reframe: "Presentations are challenging for me, but each one is practice that helps me improve."

Benefit: Rewires habitual thought patterns through conscious reframing.

5. Morning Pages

Purpose: Start the day with clarity.

Practice (popularized by Julia Cameron in *The Artist's Way*):

- Write three pages of longhand, stream-of-consciousness writing each morning.
- Do not edit or analyze—just write until pages are full.

Benefit: Clears overnight residue, reducing morning overthinking and sparking creativity.

6. The "Letter You Don't Send"

Purpose: Process unresolved emotions or conflicts.

Practice:

- Write a letter to someone expressing everything you feel— anger, hurt, love, or regret.
- Do not send it. Destroy it afterward if desired.

Benefit: Provides emotional release without the risks of confrontation.

7. The Problem-Solving Journal

Purpose: Move from looping to action.

Practice:

- Identify the problem in writing.
- Brainstorm possible solutions without judgment.
- Select one step to try and commit to it.

Benefit: Shifts the mind from circular thought to constructive problem-solving.

8. The Evening Reflection

Purpose: Release the day and prepare for rest.

Practice:

- Write: "What went well today? What challenged me? What do I release tonight?"
- End with one intention for tomorrow.

Benefit: Reduces nighttime rumination and promotes restful sleep.

Real-World Case Study: The Anxious Student

Maria, a university student, struggled with nighttime overthinking. She lay awake replaying conversations and worrying about exams. A counselor introduced her to the worry dump technique. Each night, Maria wrote her worries and separated them into controllable and uncontrollable. Over time, her anxiety decreased, and her sleep improved. Journaling gave her a container for thoughts instead of letting them spiral endlessly.

Overcoming Resistance to Journaling

Many people resist journaling, believing it requires writing skill or extensive time. In truth, journaling is about process, not product. Even one sentence—"I feel anxious today, and that's okay"—can provide relief. The key is consistency, not length.

Another resistance is fear of confronting emotions. Some worry that writing about feelings will intensify them. Research shows the opposite: expressing emotions in writing reduces their intensity and prevents long-term rumination.

How to Make Journaling a Habit

1. **Set a Regular Time**: Morning or evening often works best.
2. **Keep Tools Accessible**: Place a notebook on your nightstand or use a digital app.
3. **Start Small**: Even five minutes daily builds momentum.
4. **Pair With Rituals**: Link journaling with tea, music, or a candle to create an inviting atmosphere.
5. **Remove Judgment**: Remind yourself that no one will read it.

The Role of Self-Compassion in Journaling

Journaling works best when approached with compassion. The goal is not to judge thoughts but to witness them. Writing with curiosity—*"Why might I be feeling this way?"*—transforms journaling into a practice of kindness toward oneself.

Real-World Example: The Leader's Clarity

David, an executive, faced overwhelming responsibilities. His mind raced with competing priorities. He adopted morning pages, writing three pages each day. At first, the writing felt chaotic, but soon patterns emerged. He realized many of his worries were about delegation. By addressing this, his stress reduced, and his leadership improved. Journaling revealed blind spots that overthinking had obscured.

The Deeper Lesson: Journaling as a Mirror

Journaling is a mirror for the mind. It reflects thoughts and emotions that otherwise remain hidden. Unlike internal loops, which distort and exaggerate, journaling provides perspective. It shows not only what is present but also what patterns repeat.

Through this mirror, we gain clarity. Loops lose power when seen clearly. Emotions lose intensity when expressed. Choices become simpler when written.

Takeaway: Write It Out, Clear It Out

Overthinking thrives in silence, but journaling gives the mind a voice. Whether through freewriting, worry dumps, gratitude, reframing, morning pages, or letters unsent, journaling clears fog and restores clarity.

It is not about writing perfectly but about writing honestly. The act itself is the release. In journaling, thoughts become manageable, emotions become lighter, and the mind becomes free.

CHAPTER 6

Minimalism for the Mind

Decluttering Your Digital Life

In past generations, clutter was mostly physical—piles of paper, overstuffed closets, crowded desks. Today, clutter has shifted. For many people, the greatest source of overwhelm is not physical but digital. Notifications, emails, social media feeds, and endless apps fill our mental space. Instead of dusty attics, we have overloaded inboxes. Instead of messy drawers, we have cluttered desktops.

Digital clutter is more insidious than physical clutter because it is invisible until it demands attention. A buzzing phone, a flashing notification, or an overflowing inbox constantly tugs at the mind. Each small tug may seem trivial, but together they create mental noise that drains clarity and focus. Decluttering your digital life is not just about organization; it is about reclaiming attention, energy, and peace of mind.

Why Digital Clutter Feels Overwhelming

The brain treats incoming information as potential opportunities or threats. Each notification triggers a release of dopamine, urging us to check. Over time, this creates compulsive habits. Psychologists call this **variable reward scheduling**—the same mechanism that makes slot machines addictive. Sometimes the notification brings something exciting, often it does not. The unpredictability keeps us hooked.

Digital clutter overwhelms because it operates on three levels:

1. **Quantity**: Too many inputs—emails, messages, alerts.
2. **Quality**: Many inputs are irrelevant or low-value.
3. **Accessibility**: Devices ensure clutter is available 24/7, making escape difficult.

The result is cognitive overload. Even when not actively engaged, the mind remains partially occupied with digital clutter, reducing clarity.

The Hidden Costs of Digital Clutter

1. **Fragmented Attention**
   Each notification pulls the brain away from deep focus. Research shows it takes up to 20 minutes to fully regain concentration after an interruption.
2. **Decision Fatigue**
   Managing hundreds of emails or deciding whether to engage with notifications depletes willpower.
3. **Reduced Creativity**
   Constant input leaves little space for the brain's default mode network to wander productively, which is essential for creativity.
4. **Stress and Anxiety**
   A cluttered inbox or chaotic feed creates a sense of incompleteness, fueling low-level stress.
5. **Lost Presence**
   Digital clutter steals attention from real-world experiences—meals, conversations, or even moments of rest.

Real-World Case Study: The Overloaded Manager

Lydia, a project manager, received over 200 emails daily, plus constant Slack messages. She checked her phone dozens of times per hour, convinced she had to stay connected. Over time, she felt constantly anxious and exhausted. After a digital decluttering process—unsubscribing from unnecessary emails, setting boundaries for notifications, and creating "no-phone" zones—her anxiety decreased. She discovered that 80% of her digital input was unnecessary. The decluttering gave her back not just time but mental peace.

Steps to Declutter Your Digital Life

1. Audit Your Inputs

Begin by identifying all digital inputs—email accounts, messaging apps, social media platforms, subscriptions, notifications. Ask: *Which of these adds real value? Which simply adds noise?*

Practical tip: Keep a one-day log of every time you check your phone or computer. The results often reveal far more clutter than expected.

2. Unsubscribe and Unfollow

Digital clutter often comes from subscriptions, newsletters, or accounts that no longer serve you. Unsubscribing reduces unnecessary input at the source.

Practice:

- Set aside 30 minutes to unsubscribe from irrelevant newsletters.
- Audit your social media: unfollow accounts that drain energy rather than inspire it.

3. Turn Off Non-Essential Notifications

Not every app deserves your attention in real time. Many apps default to push notifications, but most are unnecessary.

Practice:

- Keep notifications only for essential apps (such as direct communication with family or work).
- Turn off all non-essential alerts—especially social media.

This transforms the device from a constant interrupter into a tool you control.

4. Organize Your Digital Spaces

Just as physical clutter overwhelms, messy digital spaces drain clarity.

- **Inbox**: Use folders, filters, or labels to sort messages. Aim for an "Inbox Zero" habit by processing daily.
- **Desktop**: Keep only essential files visible. Use folders to organize others.
- **Phone**: Remove rarely used apps. Group remaining apps into categories. Place distracting apps out of immediate sight.

5. Create Tech-Free Zones and Times

Constant availability fuels clutter. By creating intentional boundaries, you allow the mind to rest.

Examples:

- No phone at the dining table.
- No screens for the first 30 minutes after waking.
- Tech-free evenings one or two days a week.

These zones and times reintroduce silence into daily life.

6. Batch Digital Activities

Instead of constantly checking emails or messages, batch them into set times. For example, check email at 10 a.m., 2 p.m., and 5 p.m. Batching prevents drip-drain of attention.

7. Use Tools to Reduce Clutter

Ironically, technology can help declutter technology. Apps like Freedom, RescueTime, or Screen Time track usage and block distractions. Filters, unsubscribe tools, and password managers simplify management.

The Psychology of Letting Go

Digital decluttering often triggers fear: *What if I miss something important?* This is the digital version of **fear of missing out (FOMO).** Yet in practice, most notifications, emails, and posts are not urgent or significant.

Reframing helps: Instead of "I might miss something," think "I am choosing to focus on what matters." Letting go of digital clutter is less about missing out and more about reclaiming attention.

Real-World Example: The Minimalist Student

Carlos, a student, realized he was spending four hours daily on social media, much of it mindless scrolling. He unfollowed distracting accounts, set a daily usage limit, and placed his phone out of reach while studying. Within weeks, he gained over 20 hours weekly. More importantly, his focus and grades improved.

The Deeper Lesson: Ownership of Attention

Decluttering your digital life is not about rejecting technology—it is about reclaiming ownership of attention. Technology is a tool; clutter arises when the tool controls us instead of the other way around.

Minimalism for the mind begins with digital minimalism: stripping away the noise to reveal space for clarity, focus, and meaningful connection.

Takeaway: Fewer Inputs, Greater Clarity

Digital clutter silently drains energy and clarity through endless notifications, emails, and feeds. By auditing inputs, unsubscribing, turning off non-essential notifications, organizing digital spaces, creating tech-free zones, batching activities, and reframing FOMO, we reduce noise and reclaim focus.

When the digital world is decluttered, the mind feels lighter. The constant tug of devices fades, replaced by presence, creativity, and calm. Decluttering your digital life is not about doing less online—it is about living more fully offline.

Creating Mental Space Through Physical Order

Our environment shapes our mind more than most people realize. A cluttered desk, a messy bedroom, or a disorganized kitchen does more than inconvenience us—it weighs on our attention and mental energy. Studies in psychology and neuroscience confirm what many have felt intuitively: physical clutter creates mental clutter. When the spaces we inhabit are chaotic, the mind struggles to focus, relax, and create.

By contrast, physical order fosters clarity. Minimalist environments reduce stress, simplify decisions, and free up cognitive resources for meaningful work and relationships. Creating mental space through physical order is not about perfection or sterile environments—it is about intentionally shaping surroundings to support peace and focus.

Why Physical Order Matters for Mental Clarity

The human brain evolved in environments of relative simplicity. Modern life, however, often floods spaces with possessions—objects on desks, clothes in closets, gadgets in drawers. While each item may be harmless alone, together they create **visual noise.**

Research by UCLA's Center on Everyday Lives of Families found that mothers' stress hormone levels (cortisol) rose when they were in cluttered environments. Neuroscientists explain that every visible object is processed subconsciously, adding to cognitive load. Even when not consciously noticed, clutter silently consumes attention.

The Psychology of Clutter

Clutter impacts the mind in three primary ways:

1. **Incomplete Signals**
   Each unfinished pile of papers or half-organized drawer sends a message of incompletion: "This is not done yet." The brain interprets this as an open loop, creating background stress.
2. **Decision Fatigue**
   More possessions mean more decisions: Where should this go? Should I keep this? What if I need it later? These micro-decisions drain energy.
3. **Identity Burden**
   Sometimes clutter reflects outdated identities—clothes we no longer wear, hobbies we no longer pursue, or possessions tied to past versions of ourselves. Keeping them weighs on the mind by anchoring us to what no longer serves us.

Real-World Case Study: The Overwhelmed Professional

Nina, a freelance designer, worked from home but found herself constantly distracted. Her desk was crowded with old projects, books she hadn't read, and gadgets she rarely used. After learning about the impact of clutter, she spent a weekend decluttering. She kept only essentials on her desk: laptop, notebook, and one inspirational item. Immediately, she felt lighter. Work sessions became smoother, and creative flow improved. She realized the clutter had been silently competing for her attention.

The Benefits of Physical Order

1. **Improved Focus**
   A tidy space reduces visual distractions, allowing deeper concentration.
2. **Reduced Stress**
   Clear environments lower cortisol and create a sense of calm.

3. **Time Savings**
   Less clutter means less time searching for items or cleaning.
4. **Enhanced Creativity**
   Order creates mental space for imagination to flourish.
5. **Greater Emotional Release**
   Letting go of possessions tied to the past creates room for new experiences.

Practical Steps for Creating Mental Space Through Order

1. Start Small, Start Visible

Begin with one visible space—your desk, nightstand, or kitchen counter. Visible order creates immediate psychological relief. Progress in one area builds momentum for others.

2. Apply the "Usefulness or Joy" Test

Ask of each item: *Does this serve a purpose? Does it bring joy?* If neither, consider letting it go. This test, popularized by Marie Kondo, simplifies decision-making.

3. Create Clear Zones

Designate specific spaces for specific activities. A desk is for work, a bed is for sleep, a dining table is for meals. Mixing zones confuses the brain and blurs focus.

4. Reduce Duplicates

Often clutter comes from excess duplicates—multiple mugs, pens, or tools. Keep your favorites and release the rest.

5. Establish "Homes" for Items

Clutter accumulates when items lack designated places. Assign a home for everything. When finished, return items to their home. This prevents clutter from building.

6. Embrace the One-Minute Rule

If a task takes less than one minute—like hanging a coat or filing a paper—do it immediately. This prevents small messes from snowballing.

7. Practice Seasonal Decluttering

Schedule regular decluttering sessions—every season or every six months. Life changes, and so should possessions.

The Emotional Side of Decluttering

Physical order is not only practical—it is emotional. Many people hold onto items out of guilt, fear, or nostalgia.

- **Guilt:** "I spent money on this, I should keep it."
- **Fear:** "I might need this someday."
- **Nostalgia:** "This reminds me of who I used to be."

Recognizing these emotions is part of the process. Letting go does not dishonor the past—it honors the present. Releasing objects tied to outdated identities creates mental freedom for new growth.

Real-World Example: The Closet Transformation

Mark, a teacher, struggled with decision fatigue each morning. His closet was filled with clothes he no longer wore, yet he still sifted through them daily. After decluttering, he reduced his wardrobe to items he actually liked and wore regularly. Morning decisions became effortless. The act of simplifying his closet freed not just time but mental energy.

The Role of Ritual in Order

Decluttering is not a one-time event—it is a ritual. Daily practices maintain clarity:

- **End-of-Day Reset:** Spend five minutes tidying your workspace.
- **Weekly Sweep:** Dedicate 15 minutes to restoring order in key areas.
- **Mindful Placement:** Place items intentionally rather than leaving them randomly.

These rituals turn order into a lifestyle rather than a chore.

Minimalism vs. Sterility

Creating order does not mean living in empty, sterile spaces. Minimalism is not about deprivation but intention. The goal is not fewer possessions for their own sake but a curated environment that supports peace and clarity. Keep what serves, release what distracts.

The Deeper Lesson: Space Is Mental Fuel

Physical order is not about aesthetics—it is about energy. Each uncluttered surface, each simplified drawer, creates space not just in the room but in the mind. The fewer distractions in the environment, the more energy is available for creativity, relationships, and presence.

When we create order outside, we create peace inside. The external and internal are inseparable.

Takeaway: Clear Space, Clear Mind

Clutter is more than stuff—it is a thief of attention and clarity. By creating physical order through small, intentional steps—starting visible, simplifying possessions, creating zones, and maintaining rituals—we free the mind from hidden burdens.

The true reward of order is not a tidy desk or a neat closet but the mental space it creates. In that space, focus sharpens, stress eases, and life feels lighter.

Information Overload: Managing Inputs Wisely

We live in the most information-rich era of human history. At any given moment, we can access libraries of knowledge, news from across the globe, and instant communication with people anywhere. While this abundance offers opportunities, it also creates a paradox: the more information we consume, the less clarity we often feel. The modern mind is not starved for input—it is drowning in it.

Information overload occurs when the amount of input exceeds the brain's ability to process it. This overload creates confusion, indecision, fatigue, and a sense of being perpetually behind. Managing inputs wisely is a key practice of mental minimalism: reducing noise, curating what matters, and creating space for reflection.

Why the Brain Overloads on Information

The human brain evolved in environments with limited data. Our ancestors made decisions based on local conditions—weather patterns, immediate dangers, small social groups. The brain is optimized to handle modest amounts of input.

Modern life, however, floods the senses. News outlets, social media feeds, podcasts, emails, texts, videos, and books bombard us daily. The brain struggles because:

1. **Working Memory is Limited**
   The average person can hold about 5–9 items in working memory at once. Beyond this, overload occurs.
2. **Novelty Hijacks Attention**
   The brain is wired to prioritize new stimuli. Constant streams of novelty—updates, notifications, breaking news—hijack attention repeatedly.
3. **Fear of Missing Out (FOMO)**
   The belief that every piece of information is essential keeps people consuming long past the point of usefulness.
4. **Analysis Paralysis**
   Too much data creates indecision. Instead of clarity, more input often leads to hesitation.

The Hidden Costs of Information Overload

1. **Reduced Focus**
   Constant intake prevents the deep concentration needed for creativity and problem-solving.
2. **Decision Fatigue**
   Excessive data complicates choices. The brain tires of weighing too many options.
3. **Superficial Understanding**
   Overconsumption often leads to skimming rather than deep learning. Knowledge remains shallow, easily forgotten.
4. **Stress and Anxiety**
   The sense of never being "caught up" creates low-level anxiety. Overload mimics urgency, even when nothing is truly urgent.
5. **Lost Presence**
   Attention consumed by endless feeds leaves less space for real-world presence—conversations, nature, or inner reflection.

Real-World Case Study: The News Cycle Trap

Amir, an engineer, began his mornings scrolling through multiple news sites and social media feeds. He felt informed but increasingly anxious. The constant stream of crises left him distracted at work and unable to relax at night. When he reduced his news intake to one reliable source for 15 minutes daily, his anxiety decreased. He realized he had confused "more information" with "better understanding."

Managing Inputs Wisely

The goal is not ignorance but intentionality. By curating inputs, we preserve clarity and focus while still staying informed.

1. Audit Your Inputs

Begin by listing all regular information sources: news outlets, podcasts, YouTube channels, newsletters, social media platforms. Ask: *Which of these truly enrich me? Which simply clutter my mind?*

This awareness often reveals dozens of inputs that consume attention without adding value.

2. Limit News Consumption

News is important but overwhelming. Most headlines repeat the same stories with minor variations, yet the emotional toll accumulates.

Practice:

- Choose one or two reliable news sources.
- Set a specific time limit daily (e.g., 20 minutes).
- Avoid doomscrolling late at night, which fuels anxiety.

3. Curate Social Media

Social media blends valuable content with endless distraction. To reduce overload:

- Unfollow accounts that drain energy.
- Follow only voices that inform, inspire, or connect meaningfully.
- Use time limits or blocking tools to prevent overuse.

4. Apply the "Just-in-Time" Principle

Consume information when it is directly relevant to action. For example, instead of reading every productivity book, read one when you are actively redesigning your schedule. This prevents learning from becoming passive consumption.

5. Prioritize Depth Over Breadth

Instead of skimming dozens of articles, choose one and study it deeply. Depth creates real understanding, while breadth often creates superficial noise.

6. Schedule Reflection Time

Information is only valuable when digested. Build pauses into your day—time to step away from inputs and reflect. Without reflection, knowledge does not become wisdom.

7. Protect Morning and Evening

The brain is most vulnerable during transitions of the day. Consuming information immediately upon waking or before sleep disrupts clarity. Protect these windows by avoiding screens and focusing on intentional rituals instead.

Real-World Example: The Student's Transformation

Lila, a graduate student, subscribed to 20 academic newsletters and followed hundreds of accounts online. She felt informed but overwhelmed. Her focus suffered. She chose to unsubscribe from most newsletters, limit herself to three academic journals, and dedicate one hour weekly to reviewing them deeply. The result: less stress, better comprehension, and more meaningful contributions to her research.

The Role of Silence and Stillness

In an overloaded world, silence becomes essential. Just as the body needs rest after exertion, the mind needs stillness after input. Moments of silence—walks without headphones, meditation, or quiet meals—allow the brain to consolidate knowledge and recover clarity.

Tools for Managing Information Flow

- **Read Later Apps**: Tools like Pocket or Instapaper save articles for intentional reading instead of impulsive scrolling.
- **RSS Feeds or Curated Digests**: Aggregate quality sources in one place instead of scattering across platforms.
- **Time-Tracking Apps**: Monitor how much time is spent consuming information to reveal patterns of overload.

The Deeper Lesson: Less Input, More Wisdom

Information does not equal wisdom. In fact, excessive information often blocks wisdom by preventing reflection. True understanding arises not from volume but from discernment—the ability to select what matters and ignore what does not.

Minimalism for the mind requires resisting the cultural pressure to consume endlessly. By curating inputs, limiting noise, and making space for silence, we transform information from a flood into a stream—nourishing, manageable, and clear.

Takeaway: Choose What Deserves Your Mind

Information overload is not solved by more tools or faster consumption but by intentionality. Audit inputs, limit news, curate social media, apply just-in-time learning, and embrace silence.

By managing inputs wisely, we protect mental space for creativity, relationships, and peace. The mind was not designed to carry the world's information every day—it was designed to live fully in the present moment. Choose what deserves your mind, and clarity will follow.

The Power of Saying "No"

One of the most underestimated skills in cultivating mental minimalism and clarity is the ability to say "no." For many people, overcommitment—not lack of opportunity—is the greatest thief of focus. Invitations, requests, responsibilities, and digital distractions all compete for attention. Without boundaries, the mind becomes cluttered with obligations, draining energy and leaving little space for creativity or peace.

Saying "no" is not simply refusal—it is the active choice to protect your time, energy, and values. Each "no" creates space for a deeper "yes" to what matters most. Yet culturally and personally, many find "no" difficult. Guilt, fear of conflict, or desire for approval lead to unnecessary commitments. Learning the power of "no" is therefore central to mental freedom.

Why "No" Feels Difficult

The reluctance to say "no" is rooted in psychology and social conditioning:

1. **Fear of Rejection**
   Humans are social beings. Saying "no" risks disapproval, which historically threatened belonging. The brain still interprets rejection as danger.
2. **People-Pleasing Tendencies**
   Many equate kindness with compliance. Saying "yes" feels like caring, even when it leads to resentment.
3. **FOMO (Fear of Missing Out)**
   Saying "no" can feel like missing opportunities. The lure of "what if" keeps people overcommitted.
4. **Identity Tied to Busyness**
   In many cultures, busyness equals importance. Saying "no" may feel like losing status.
5. **Unclear Priorities**
   Without clarity on values, it is difficult to evaluate requests, leading to default "yes" responses.

The Hidden Costs of Always Saying "Yes"

While saying yes may feel easier in the moment, the long-term costs are significant:

- **Diluted Focus**: Spreading energy across too many commitments prevents depth in any.
- **Resentment**: Obligations accepted reluctantly often breed frustration.
- **Burnout**: Overcommitment leads to exhaustion, both physical and mental.
- **Loss of Autonomy**: Life becomes driven by others' agendas rather than personal values.
- **Reduced Growth**: Time spent on low-value commitments displaces time for high-value growth.

Real-World Case Study: The Overcommitted Volunteer

Samantha, a teacher, agreed to every request—from leading committees to organizing events. While admired for her dedication, she became overwhelmed, exhausted, and resentful. After working with a mentor, she began practicing "no" by aligning commitments with her values: teaching and mentoring students. She released committee work and non-essential obligations. The result was greater energy for her true passion, and her impact actually grew.

Reframing "No"

To embrace the power of "no," it must be reframed:

- **"No" is Not Rejection**: It is refusal of a request, not rejection of a person.
- **"No" is Self-Care**: Protecting mental space ensures sustainability and generosity.
- **"No" Creates Space for "Yes"**: Each no to distraction is a yes to focus. Each no to obligation is a yes to freedom.

Practical Strategies for Saying "No"

1. Clarify Priorities

Without clarity, all requests feel equally important. Define core values and goals. When a request arises, ask: *Does this align with my priorities?* If not, say no.

2. Use the "Hell Yes or No" Rule

Author Derek Sivers suggests: If something does not excite you as a "hell yes," consider it a no. This prevents lukewarm commitments that drain energy.

3. Delay Your Response

Instead of defaulting to yes, create a pause: *"Let me check my schedule and get back to you."* This provides space to evaluate alignment.

4. Practice Polite, Clear Refusals

"No" does not require hostility. Clear, respectful language works best:

- "I appreciate the offer, but I can't commit right now."
- "This isn't the right fit for me, though I wish you success."
- "Thank you for thinking of me, but I need to focus on other priorities."

5. Set Boundaries in Advance

Establishing boundaries prevents constant negotiation. Examples:

- No work emails after 7 p.m.
- Only two social commitments per week.
- No phone use during meals.

Clear boundaries reduce decision fatigue and normalize saying no.

6. Use Substitutes

Sometimes a full no is unnecessary—offering alternatives preserves relationships:

- "I can't attend, but I can recommend someone who may help."
- "I can't join now, but let's reconnect next month."

7. Strengthen the "No" Muscle

Start with small nos. Decline a subscription, an unnecessary purchase, or a minor social invitation. With practice, the ability to say no grows stronger.

Real-World Example: The Entrepreneur's Boundary

Daniel, a startup founder, initially said yes to every networking event and collaboration. He soon became exhausted, with little time for his company. By applying the "hell yes or no" rule, he cut commitments by half. This allowed him to focus on his product, which flourished. The strategic nos fueled his most important yes.

The Emotional Aftermath of Saying "No"

At first, saying no may bring guilt. This is natural but temporary. Over time, as the benefits of clarity and reduced stress appear, guilt diminishes. Remind yourself: every no protects the energy to say yes more deeply elsewhere.

The Deeper Lesson: Saying No as an Act of Freedom

Minimalism for the mind is not only about physical or digital decluttering—it is about boundary clarity. Without the ability to say no, external demands shape life. With it, we reclaim authorship.

Saying no is not selfish—it is responsible. It ensures our time and energy are invested where they matter most, rather than scattered across obligations that leave us drained.

Takeaway: Boundaries Create Space for Growth

The power of saying "no" lies in its ability to protect clarity, focus, and well-being. By clarifying priorities, practicing respectful refusal, delaying responses, and setting boundaries, we gain the courage to decline what does not serve us.

Each no creates space for a deeper yes—to our values, to our passions, to our growth. Mental minimalism begins not only with what we release but also with what we refuse to take on. Saying no is the key that unlocks mental freedom.

Designing a Low-Stress Lifestyle

Stress is often treated as an unavoidable part of modern life. Deadlines, financial pressures, social obligations, and constant digital noise make stress seem inevitable. Yet while we cannot eliminate every challenge, we can design lifestyles that reduce unnecessary stress and build resilience for what remains.

A low-stress lifestyle does not mean avoiding effort or responsibility. It means intentionally creating rhythms, environments, and habits that minimize avoidable tension and maximize mental freedom. By aligning choices with values, simplifying routines, and cultivating balance, we reduce the mental clutter that fuels overwhelm.

Why Lifestyle Matters More Than Quick Fixes

Many people treat stress reactively: they use relaxation techniques, vacations, or weekend escapes to recover. While helpful, these are temporary fixes. If the lifestyle itself constantly generates stress, relief will always be short-lived.

Lifestyle design addresses the root. By embedding simplicity, balance, and clarity into daily routines, stress decreases not occasionally but consistently. This is the essence of minimalism for the mind: structuring life itself to support peace.

The Science of Stress and Lifestyle

Stress triggers the release of cortisol and adrenaline, preparing the body for fight-or-flight. Short bursts can be motivating, but chronic activation harms health—weakening immunity, impairing memory, and increasing risk of anxiety and depression.

Lifestyle is a powerful moderator. Diet, sleep, environment, relationships, and routines influence how often stress is triggered and how quickly recovery occurs. Thought loops may amplify stress, but lifestyle sets the stage.

Core Principles of a Low-Stress Lifestyle

1. Simplicity Over Complexity

Every added layer of complexity—extra possessions, commitments, or inputs—creates more decisions and potential stress. Simplifying choices reduces overwhelm.

Practical Example: Instead of maintaining three email accounts, consolidate into one. Instead of chasing every new hobby, focus on one or two that truly nourish.

2. Rhythms Over Chaos

Unpredictability fuels stress. Consistent daily rhythms—wake times, meals, exercise—create stability. The brain relaxes when life has reliable structure.

Practical Example: A consistent morning routine signals the brain to prepare for focus. A nightly ritual signals rest. These rhythms reduce anxiety by removing uncertainty.

3. Boundaries Over Overcommitment

As explored earlier, stress often comes from saying yes too often. Boundaries prevent overload and protect energy.

Practical Example: No emails after 7 p.m. ensures evenings are for rest, not work anxiety.

4. Environment Over Willpower

Stress is easier to manage by shaping environments than by relying on willpower. An uncluttered home, organized workspace, or nature exposure reduces triggers without effort.

Practical Example: Removing the TV from the bedroom reduces late-night overstimulation, improving rest without needing constant discipline.

5. Recovery Over Constant Drive

High performance requires recovery. Without breaks, the nervous system remains in stress mode. Designing daily pauses prevents burnout.

Practical Example: Scheduling a 10-minute walk between meetings resets attention and lowers cortisol.

Practical Steps to Design a Low-Stress Lifestyle

Step 1: Audit Stressors

List recurring sources of stress. Separate them into:

- Avoidable stress (unnecessary commitments, clutter, digital overload).
- Unavoidable stress (work deadlines, caregiving, major transitions).

Focus first on reducing avoidable stress—it often represents the majority.

Step 2: Simplify Daily Choices

Decision fatigue magnifies stress. Automate or simplify where possible:

- Meal prep to reduce food decisions.
- Capsule wardrobes to simplify outfits.
- Fixed exercise times to avoid scheduling conflict.

Step 3: Protect Key Foundations

Three lifestyle foundations reduce stress across the board:

- **Sleep**: Consistent schedules and screen-free nights.
- **Movement**: Daily activity reduces cortisol.
- **Nutrition**: Balanced meals stabilize mood and energy.

When these are stable, resilience to other stressors increases.

Step 4: Redesign Your Environment

Physical surroundings influence stress levels.

- Declutter spaces to reduce visual noise.
- Introduce calming elements like plants, natural light, or soothing colors.
- Create dedicated zones for work, rest, and leisure to reduce blurred boundaries.

Step 5: Establish Micro-Rituals of Calm

Embed short practices into daily life:

- Morning breathing to set calm intention.
- Midday gratitude to shift perspective.
- Evening journaling to release tension.

These rituals prevent stress buildup.

Step 6: Align Commitments With Values

Stress often arises from misaligned obligations. Ask: *Does this commitment reflect my core values?* If not, release or renegotiate it.

Step 7: Embrace "Good Enough"

Perfectionism fuels chronic stress. Accepting "good enough" in areas that don't require perfection frees energy. Reserve excellence for what matters most.

Real-World Case Study: The High-Performing Executive

Arjun, a corporate executive, lived in constant stress—late nights, endless emails, no downtime. Burnout loomed. Through lifestyle redesign, he simplified his wardrobe, restricted emails to three windows per day, and scheduled daily walks. He also set a strict boundary: weekends were family-only. Stress levels dropped dramatically, yet his work performance improved. The change was not in working less but in working with clarity.

The Role of Relationships

No lifestyle design is complete without attention to relationships. Supportive connections buffer stress, while toxic ones amplify it. Cultivating uplifting relationships, setting boundaries with draining ones, and practicing open communication are vital for mental freedom.

The Importance of Restorative Activities

Low-stress lifestyles include regular practices that restore joy: reading, cooking, art, nature walks, or simply quiet reflection. These are not luxuries but necessities, balancing the demands of modern life.

The Deeper Lesson: Lifestyle as a Form of Mental Architecture

Just as architecture shapes how people move through buildings, lifestyle design shapes how the mind moves through life. Cluttered lifestyles create constant friction; simplified ones create flow. A low-stress lifestyle is not accidental—it is constructed, choice by choice, boundary by boundary, rhythm by rhythm.

Takeaway: Build Life Around Clarity, Not Chaos

Stress will always exist, but much of it is optional. By simplifying routines, creating rhythms, protecting foundations, shaping environments, and aligning commitments with values, we design lifestyles that reduce unnecessary stress and build resilience for challenges.

The essence of minimalism for the mind is not deprivation but design: creating a life where clarity is the default, not the exception. With each intentional choice, we move from a reactive life of stress to a deliberate life of freedom.

CHAPTER 7

Emotional Intelligence as Mental Freedom

Understanding Emotional Triggers

Few things disrupt mental clarity more suddenly than emotional triggers. One moment, you may feel calm and composed; the next, a comment, tone of voice, or even a memory sparks irritation, sadness, or fear. Triggers are those specific stimuli that activate strong emotional reactions, often disproportionate to the situation.

Everyone has triggers. They might arise in relationships, at work, or in moments of stress. While some triggers are obvious, many are subtle—slight cues that set off waves of overreaction without conscious awareness. Understanding emotional triggers is therefore foundational to emotional intelligence and mental freedom. When we learn to identify, interpret, and manage triggers, we reclaim the ability to respond consciously rather than react impulsively.

What Are Emotional Triggers?

An emotional trigger is an external event or internal thought that activates an intense emotional response. The key features of triggers are:

1. **Disproportionate Intensity**
   The reaction is stronger than the situation alone seems to justify.
2. **Automatic Response**
   The reaction arises quickly, often bypassing rational thought.
3. **Personal History**
   Triggers are usually rooted in past experiences, often connected to unresolved wounds, insecurities, or conditioning.

For example:

- A colleague's criticism may trigger anger because it echoes childhood experiences of harsh judgment.

- Being excluded from an event may trigger sadness tied to past feelings of rejection.
- Sudden changes may trigger anxiety for someone whose past included instability.

The Neuroscience of Triggers

Triggers activate the **amygdala**, the brain's emotional alarm system. When the amygdala perceives threat—whether physical or psychological—it floods the body with stress hormones like cortisol and adrenaline. This prepares the body for fight, flight, or freeze.

The prefrontal cortex, responsible for reasoning and perspective, is temporarily bypassed. This explains why triggered responses often feel irrational: the brain is prioritizing survival over logic.

While this system once protected humans from predators, today it is often activated by social or emotional cues, leading to unnecessary reactivity.

Why Triggers Persist

Triggers remain powerful because they are linked to unresolved emotional memories. The brain encodes not just facts but also the emotions tied to them. When a present situation resembles a past wound, the brain reacts as if the original wound is happening again.

For example, someone who was frequently abandoned in childhood may feel overwhelming fear if a partner shows signs of withdrawal. The intensity of the reaction is less about the present event and more about the unresolved past.

Common Types of Triggers

1. **Criticism**: Feeling attacked or devalued.
2. **Rejection**: Being excluded or ignored.
3. **Loss of Control**: Situations that feel unpredictable.

4. **Injustice**: Perceived unfairness.
5. **Comparison**: Seeing oneself as less successful than others.
6. **Abandonment**: Fear of being left behind.
7. **Failure**: Situations that suggest inadequacy.

Recognizing which triggers affect you most is the first step toward managing them.

Real-World Case Study: The Triggered Manager

Elena, a manager, often felt enraged when team members questioned her decisions. She later realized her anger was not about the questions but about childhood experiences of being dismissed by her parents. Each question unconsciously echoed that pain. By recognizing the trigger, Elena learned to pause, breathe, and respond calmly. Her leadership improved, and her team felt more comfortable collaborating.

Strategies to Understand and Manage Triggers

1. Build Self-Awareness

Notice patterns. Ask: *When do I feel sudden emotional intensity? What situations provoke strong reactions?* Journaling helps identify recurring triggers.

2. Pause Before Reacting

When triggered, create space before responding. Techniques include:

- Counting to ten.
- Taking slow breaths.
- Physically stepping away.

This pause re-engages the prefrontal cortex, allowing rational thought to return.

3. Trace the Root

Ask: *What past experience might this trigger connect to?* Identifying the root transforms the trigger from mystery to signal.

4. Reframe the Story

Triggers often arise from distorted interpretations. For example, criticism may feel like rejection but may simply be feedback. Reframing reduces emotional intensity.

5. Develop Coping Rituals

Personal rituals—like a mantra ("I am safe"), grounding techniques, or physical movement—help regulate triggered emotions.

6. Communicate Triggers in Relationships

Sharing triggers with trusted people reduces misunderstandings. For example: *"I sometimes get defensive when I feel criticized. If you can phrase feedback gently, it helps me respond better."*

7. Practice Self-Compassion

Triggers often bring shame: *Why am I overreacting?* Self-compassion reframes this: *I am reacting strongly because of old wounds, and I am learning to heal.*

Real-World Example: The Relationship Trigger

Jon often felt abandoned when his partner worked late. He accused her of neglect, which caused conflict. Through reflection, Jon recognized the trigger was tied to childhood abandonment by a parent. With awareness, he began practicing grounding techniques when his partner was late. He also communicated his feelings openly. The trigger did not vanish, but it no longer controlled his reactions.

Triggers as Teachers

While uncomfortable, triggers can be powerful teachers. Each one points to an unresolved wound or unmet need. Instead of seeing triggers as enemies, we can view them as guides showing where healing is needed.

For instance, repeated anger at unfairness may point to a deep value of justice. Repeated sadness at rejection may point to a need for belonging. By addressing the need, we reduce the power of the trigger.

The Deeper Lesson: From Reaction to Response

Understanding triggers is not about eliminating emotions—it is about reclaiming choice. When we are unaware, triggers control us. When we are aware, we control our response.

Triggers remind us that mental freedom requires emotional freedom. By identifying, tracing, reframing, and communicating triggers, we move from unconscious reaction to conscious response.

Takeaway: Awareness Turns Triggers into Signals

Emotional triggers may feel like sudden storms, but they are signals, not destiny. They reveal where past wounds still echo in the present. By approaching them with awareness, compassion, and strategy, we reduce their power.

The more we understand triggers, the more freedom we gain to live with clarity and intentionality. In mastering triggers, we master not just reactions but life itself.

Self-Awareness: The Foundation of EQ

Emotional intelligence (EQ) is often described as the ability to recognize, understand, and manage emotions—both in ourselves and in others. At its core, however, all aspects of EQ rest on one foundational skill: **self-awareness.** Without awareness of our own emotions, thoughts, and patterns, we cannot regulate ourselves, empathize with others, or respond intentionally. Self-awareness is the gateway to mental freedom.

While many people believe they are self-aware, research suggests otherwise. A study by organizational psychologist Tasha Eurich found that while 95% of people think they are self-aware, only about 10–15% actually demonstrate strong self-awareness. This gap explains why so many intelligent, capable individuals struggle with relationships, decision-making, or stress management—they are operating with blind spots.

Cultivating self-awareness is therefore not optional. It is the foundation upon which clarity, resilience, and emotional growth are built.

What Is Self-Awareness?

Self-awareness is the ability to consciously observe our internal state—our emotions, thoughts, and behaviors—and to understand how they influence both ourselves and others. It has two dimensions:

1. **Internal Self-Awareness**
   Recognizing our own emotions, strengths, weaknesses, values, and triggers.
2. **External Self-Awareness**
   Understanding how others perceive us and how our actions impact them.

Balanced self-awareness requires both: knowing ourselves and recognizing our effects on the world.

Why Self-Awareness Is Essential for Emotional Intelligence

Every other component of EQ—self-regulation, empathy, social skills—depends on awareness. For example:

- Without awareness of anger rising, we cannot regulate it before it explodes.
- Without awareness of personal values, we cannot make aligned decisions.
- Without awareness of how our words land, we cannot build trust in relationships.

Self-awareness creates the space between stimulus and response. It allows us to pause, reflect, and choose rather than react automatically.

The Neuroscience of Self-Awareness

Neuroscientific research shows that self-awareness involves activity in the **prefrontal cortex**, particularly the medial prefrontal cortex, which processes self-referential thoughts. Mindfulness practices that cultivate awareness reduce amygdala reactivity (emotional overdrive) and increase prefrontal regulation.

In other words, awareness literally rewires the brain to move from reactivity to reflection.

The Blind Spot Problem

One of the greatest barriers to self-awareness is blind spots— patterns that are obvious to others but invisible to us. Blind spots often involve:

- Defensive habits (interrupting, blaming, avoiding conflict).
- Emotional triggers (overreacting in specific situations).
- Contradictions between stated values and actual behavior.

Blind spots persist because the mind prefers comfort to truth. Facing them requires courage and feedback.

Real-World Case Study: The Unaware Leader

Thomas, a team leader, prided himself on being approachable. Yet his staff described him as intimidating and dismissive. He was shocked when he received anonymous feedback. His blind spot was tone—while he saw himself as direct, others perceived him as harsh. By cultivating self-awareness through feedback and reflection, Thomas adjusted his communication, improving morale and trust.

Practical Tools to Build Self-Awareness

1. Mindful Pause

Pause regularly to ask: *What am I feeling right now? What thoughts are present? How is my body reacting?* This simple check-in interrupts autopilot and brings hidden states into awareness.

2. Emotion Labeling

Research shows that labeling emotions reduces their intensity. Instead of "I feel bad," specify: "I feel anxious because of uncertainty." Clarity transforms vague overwhelm into something manageable.

3. Journaling

Writing thoughts and feelings externalizes them, revealing patterns. Over time, journaling shows recurring triggers, themes, and blind spots.

4. Feedback Seeking

Ask trusted colleagues, friends, or mentors: *How do you experience me in conversations? Where might I have blind spots?* External feedback expands self-awareness beyond internal reflection.

5. Meditation and Breathwork

Mindfulness meditation trains awareness of thoughts and feelings without judgment. Breathwork reconnects body awareness with mental state. Both practices strengthen the neural pathways of awareness.

6. Triggers Log

Keep a log of moments of strong emotional reaction. Record the situation, the trigger, the feeling, and the response. Over time, patterns emerge, deepening understanding.

Internal vs. External Self-Awareness

It is possible to excel in one dimension and lack the other. For example:

- Someone highly reflective (internal) may misjudge how others perceive them (external).
- Someone highly aware of how others see them may neglect their own emotions or values.

Balanced growth requires both looking inward and listening outward.

Real-World Example: The Athlete's Awareness

Lena, a professional athlete, noticed she often felt nervous before games but couldn't articulate why. Through journaling and mindfulness, she realized the anxiety came from fear of disappointing her coach, not from the game itself. By naming and addressing this, her performance improved. Awareness gave her freedom from misplaced fear.

Barriers to Self-Awareness

1. **Ego Defense**: Admitting flaws threatens identity.
2. **Busyness**: Constant activity leaves no space for reflection.
3. **Cultural Conditioning**: Some cultures discourage open discussion of emotions.
4. **Fear of Vulnerability**: Awareness brings uncomfortable truths.

Overcoming these barriers requires courage, humility, and safe spaces for reflection.

The Deeper Lesson: Awareness Precedes Change

Self-awareness is not about self-criticism. It is about clarity. You cannot change what you cannot see. By shining light on emotions, habits, and patterns, you create the possibility of choice. Without awareness, life is lived on autopilot, ruled by triggers and blind spots. With awareness, life becomes intentional.

Takeaway: Know Yourself, Free Yourself

Self-awareness is the foundation of emotional intelligence and mental freedom. By practicing mindful pauses, labeling emotions, journaling, seeking feedback, and embracing reflection, we learn to see ourselves clearly.

Awareness does not eliminate flaws or emotions—it transforms our relationship to them. In knowing ourselves, we gain the power to regulate, empathize, and grow. Mental freedom begins with this simple truth: to change the mind, we must first observe it.

Empathy Without Emotional Burden

Empathy is often celebrated as one of the most important human qualities. It allows us to connect, understand, and support others. But empathy, when unbalanced, can become overwhelming. Many people who pride themselves on being empathetic find themselves exhausted, burdened by the emotions of others, or unable to separate their own feelings from the struggles around them.

True empathy does not mean carrying every emotional weight. It means understanding another's perspective while maintaining clarity and boundaries. When practiced wisely, empathy strengthens relationships and emotional intelligence. When practiced without balance, it drains mental energy and erodes freedom. Learning empathy without emotional burden is therefore essential for sustaining both compassion and mental clarity.

What Is Empathy?

Empathy involves sensing, understanding, and sometimes sharing the emotions of others. Psychologists identify three main forms:

1. **Cognitive Empathy**: Understanding what someone else is thinking or feeling.
2. **Emotional Empathy**: Feeling what another person feels, often at a visceral level.
3. **Compassionate Empathy**: Combining understanding and feeling with a desire to help.

Each form has value, but emotional empathy—feeling others' pain directly—can become overwhelming if not balanced with boundaries.

The Neuroscience of Empathy

Empathy activates the **mirror neuron system**, a network of brain cells that fire both when we act and when we observe others acting.

This explains why seeing someone cry can make us feel sadness or why watching pain on screen can cause discomfort in our own bodies.

While this system fosters connection, it also explains emotional overload. Too much mirroring blurs the boundary between self and other, leading to what researchers call **empathic distress.**

The Difference Between Empathy and Sympathy

Empathy often gets confused with sympathy. Sympathy involves feeling *for* someone ("I feel sorry for you"), while empathy involves feeling *with* someone ("I understand your pain"). Sympathy can create distance, while empathy creates connection. Yet empathy without boundaries can lead to absorption of others' suffering.

The balance lies in compassionate empathy: connecting deeply but retaining enough perspective to remain grounded.

The Hidden Costs of Unbalanced Empathy

1. **Emotional Exhaustion**
   Taking on others' emotions leads to compassion fatigue, especially in caregivers, therapists, or empathetic friends.
2. **Blurred Identity**
   Without boundaries, empathetic people may lose touch with their own needs and feelings.
3. **Ineffective Help**
   Over-identifying with pain can make us less helpful, because we are overwhelmed rather than constructive.
4. **Resentment**
   Carrying others' burdens without balance can create frustration and distance.

Real-World Case Study: The Compassion Fatigue Nurse

Rachel, a nurse, entered healthcare out of deep empathy. She listened intently to patients and absorbed their fears and grief. Over time, she became emotionally exhausted, dreading shifts. A mentor taught her to practice boundaries: being fully present during interactions, then intentionally releasing emotions afterward. By shifting to compassionate empathy, Rachel regained energy and sustained her calling.

How to Practice Empathy Without Emotional Burden

1. Differentiate Self From Other

Remind yourself: *Their emotions are theirs, not mine.* You can understand and support without carrying. Visualizations help— imagine their emotions as a passing cloud rather than a weight you must hold.

2. Use Grounding Techniques

When feeling overwhelmed, ground yourself:

- Notice physical sensations (feet on the floor, breath in the body).
- Name your own emotion: *"I feel anxious right now, but this anxiety belongs to me, not to them."*
- Create a mental boundary: *"I can care without absorbing."*

3. Shift From Emotional Empathy to Compassionate Empathy

Emotional empathy absorbs; compassionate empathy connects with the intention to help. Ask: *What is one way I can support without losing myself?* Sometimes this means listening; other times, offering perspective or action.

4. Practice Detachment With Care

Detachment is not indifference. It is the ability to remain present while keeping perspective. Like a therapist who listens deeply but does not take problems home, we can practice engaged detachment.

5. Build Emotional Recovery Rituals

After emotionally intense interactions, practice rituals to release absorbed energy:

- Journaling feelings.
- Taking a walk in nature.
- Practicing breathwork or meditation.
- Symbolically washing hands or shaking off tension.

These rituals signal the mind to release what is not yours.

6. Set Clear Boundaries

Empathy without boundaries leads to exploitation. Boundaries can be verbal ("I want to support you, but I can't take calls late at night") or internal (deciding what emotional weight you will and won't carry). Boundaries make empathy sustainable.

7. Strengthen Self-Compassion

Empathy begins with self. Without compassion for your own limits, empathy turns to burden. Self-compassion practices—speaking kindly to yourself, honoring needs, accepting imperfection—protect against burnout.

Real-World Example: The Friend Who Carried Too Much

Miguel prided himself on being the "go-to friend." Everyone confided in him. But he became overwhelmed, carrying others' heartbreaks, family dramas, and stress. He realized he was saying yes to every emotional demand without limits. By learning to listen supportively but redirect when needed, Miguel found balance. He remained empathetic but no longer exhausted.

The Role of Perspective in Healthy Empathy

Perspective-taking transforms empathy. Instead of drowning in another's pain, we view it through a wider lens:

- *"They are suffering now, but suffering can change."*
- *"This difficulty may be their opportunity for growth."*

This perspective allows connection without despair.

The Deeper Lesson: Empathy as Connection, Not Absorption

Empathy is not about carrying every burden—it is about seeing and honoring another's humanity. The difference lies in boundaries. Without them, empathy drains. With them, empathy uplifts.

When empathy is balanced, it enriches both giver and receiver. It strengthens connection without eroding self. It becomes a source of compassion rather than fatigue.

Takeaway: Care Deeply, Stand Firmly

Empathy without boundaries is emotional entanglement. Empathy with awareness is connection. By differentiating self from other, grounding, shifting to compassionate empathy, setting boundaries, and practicing recovery rituals, we care without being consumed.

The true power of empathy lies not in burden but in balance. When we care deeply while standing firmly, we sustain compassion—and preserve our mental freedom.

Respond vs. React: Mastering the Gap

In the space of a few seconds, the course of an interaction—or even a relationship—can change dramatically. A harsh word from a colleague, a child's tantrum, a partner's criticism: these moments trigger immediate impulses. Often, we react—snapping back, shutting down, or making rash decisions—before thinking. Later, regret follows.

But there is another way: responding. Unlike reaction, which is impulsive and automatic, a response is thoughtful and intentional. The difference lies in a small but powerful pause—a gap between stimulus and action. Mastering this gap is one of the most important skills of emotional intelligence and mental freedom.

Reaction vs. Response: The Core Difference

- **Reaction**: Immediate, emotional, unconscious. Driven by the amygdala and survival instincts. Often escalates conflict or creates regret.
- **Response**: Deliberate, reflective, conscious. Involves the prefrontal cortex and higher reasoning. Focused on long-term values rather than short-term impulses.

For example, if criticized in a meeting:

- A reaction might be snapping defensively, escalating tension.
- A response might be pausing, asking clarifying questions, and addressing the issue calmly.

The event is the same, but the outcomes diverge entirely.

The Neuroscience of the Gap

When triggered, the amygdala activates the fight-flight-freeze response. This shuts down parts of the prefrontal cortex responsible for reasoning. Reactions happen in milliseconds. However, research shows that practices like mindfulness increase the activity of the prefrontal cortex, strengthening the brain's ability to pause and regulate impulses.

This pause—the gap—is the key. Austrian neurologist Viktor Frankl famously wrote: *"Between stimulus and response there is a space. In that space is our power to choose our response. In our response lies our growth and our freedom."*

Why We Default to Reaction

1. **Evolutionary Survival**: Quick reactions once protected us from predators.
2. **Emotional Triggers**: Past wounds amplify sensitivity to certain cues.
3. **Stress and Fatigue**: Exhaustion reduces the brain's regulatory power, making reactions more likely.
4. **Cultural Conditioning**: Many environments reward quick retorts or assertiveness without reflection.

The Costs of Reactivity

- **Damaged Relationships**: Reacting in anger or defensiveness erodes trust.
- **Poor Decisions**: Impulsive choices often neglect long-term consequences.
- **Escalated Conflict**: Reactions fuel cycles of blame and retaliation.
- **Regret and Shame**: Many people later regret words spoken in reactivity.

Real-World Case Study: The Customer Service Trigger

James, a customer service representative, often reacted defensively when customers complained. He took criticism personally, escalating conflicts. After training in mindfulness, he began pausing before responding. He listened actively, validated concerns, and then addressed issues. Customer satisfaction improved, and James felt less stressed. The difference was not in the complaints but in mastering the gap.

Strategies to Master the Gap

1. Practice the Pause

When triggered, resist the urge to act immediately. Even a two-second pause can allow the prefrontal cortex to re-engage. Techniques include:

- Taking one deep breath.
- Counting to three before replying.
- Silently repeating a grounding phrase: *"Choose calm."*

2. Label the Emotion

Naming emotions reduces their intensity. Instead of unconsciously reacting, say internally: *"I feel angry."* This acknowledgment shifts the brain from reaction to awareness.

3. Ask Grounding Questions

When triggered, ask:

- *What is happening here?*
- *What matters most in this situation?*
- *How will I feel about this choice tomorrow?*

Questions redirect attention from impulse to perspective.

4. Create Response Rituals

Develop rituals that help regulate before responding:

- Step away for a moment.
- Write a draft response but don't send immediately.

- Drink water or stretch briefly.

These rituals create a natural gap for reflection.

5. Anchor in Values

Responses rooted in values create long-term clarity. When tempted to react defensively, ask: *What response aligns with my values— respect, patience, integrity?* Values anchor behavior beyond the heat of emotion.

6. Train Through Mindfulness

Mindfulness strengthens the brain's ability to notice impulses without acting on them. Regular practice increases self-regulation, making the pause more natural in daily life.

7. Use After-Action Reflection

When you react impulsively, reflect afterward: *What triggered me? What could I have done differently?* Over time, reflection builds awareness and prepares the mind to respond better next time.

Real-World Example: The Parenting Gap

Sophia, a mother, often reacted harshly when her children refused to listen. She later felt guilty. Through practice, she began pausing, taking a deep breath, and lowering her tone. Instead of shouting, she calmly explained expectations. Her children became more cooperative, and her guilt decreased. Mastering the gap transformed not only her behavior but her relationship with her children.

Responding Under Pressure

High-stress environments—boardrooms, emergencies, conflicts— challenge the ability to pause. Yet these are the moments where mastering the gap matters most. Elite athletes, military leaders, and negotiators train specifically to regulate emotions under pressure, proving that responding instead of reacting is a skill that can be cultivated.

Barriers to Mastering the Gap

1. **Impatience**: Believing quickness equals strength.
2. **Ego**: Wanting to win arguments rather than resolve them.
3. **Habit**: Years of reactive patterns make responses feel unnatural at first.

Overcoming these barriers requires persistence and self-compassion.

The Deeper Lesson: Freedom Lies in the Pause

Reactions are chains, binding us to old patterns. Responses are freedom, allowing us to choose anew. The difference is a moment of awareness—a breath, a pause, a question.

Mastering the gap transforms life: arguments become dialogues, crises become manageable, and regret gives way to integrity. This is not about suppressing emotion but directing it wisely.

Takeaway: Pause, Then Choose

The gap between stimulus and action is small but powerful. In that pause lies the choice between reaction and response. By practicing pauses, labeling emotions, grounding, creating rituals, anchoring in values, and training through mindfulness, we master this gap.

The gift of this mastery is freedom: the freedom to respond with clarity rather than react with impulse, the freedom to live by choice rather than habit.

Building Resilience Through Reframing

Resilience is not the absence of hardship but the ability to recover, adapt, and even grow from it. Everyone faces setbacks—failure, rejection, loss, uncertainty. The difference between those who crumble under adversity and those who emerge stronger lies not in what happens to them, but in how they interpret what happens.

This is where **reframing** becomes central. Resilience is not only physical toughness or blind optimism. It is the mental flexibility to see challenges through a constructive lens. By consciously reframing experiences, we shift from seeing obstacles as threats to viewing them as opportunities for growth. This skill transforms adversity into a source of strength rather than suffering.

The Psychology of Resilience

Psychologists define resilience as the ability to bounce back after difficulty. It involves adaptability, perseverance, and emotional regulation. Research shows that resilient people are not free from pain; rather, they are skilled at processing pain in ways that preserve hope.

Cognitive appraisal theory explains this well: our reaction to events depends less on the events themselves and more on how we appraise them. The same setback—say, losing a job—can be framed as devastating failure or as an opportunity for reinvention. The event is the same; the meaning makes the difference.

Why Reframing Builds Resilience

Reframing strengthens resilience because it:

1. **Reduces Emotional Intensity**
   Viewing stressors differently lowers anxiety and fear.

2. **Restores Agency**
Reframing shifts focus from what we cannot control to what we can influence.
3. **Fosters Growth Mindset**
Seeing challenges as learning opportunities promotes persistence.
4. **Creates Hope**
Reframing allows for possibility, preventing despair.

The Neuroscience of Reframing Resilience

Studies using brain imaging show that reframing activates the prefrontal cortex, calming the amygdala's stress response. This explains why resilient individuals often appear calm in crisis: they are not denying difficulty but regulating how they perceive it. Over time, repeated reframing builds new neural pathways, making resilience more natural.

Common Situations Where Reframing Builds Resilience

1. **Failure**
Reframe: Failure as feedback. Each mistake is a teacher, guiding the next attempt.
2. **Rejection**
Reframe: Rejection as redirection. Closed doors point toward better-fitting opportunities.
3. **Uncertainty**
Reframe: Uncertainty as possibility. Not knowing the outcome also means new outcomes are possible.
4. **Loss**
Reframe: Loss as reminder. While grief is real, loss can deepen gratitude for what remains.
5. **Stress**
Reframe: Stress as signal. Stress often highlights what matters most, guiding priorities.

Real-World Case Study: The Resilient Entrepreneur

Amira, an entrepreneur, launched a business that failed within a year. Initially devastated, she reframed the experience: rather than seeing herself as a failure, she saw the venture as a classroom. She analyzed mistakes, learned about leadership, and launched a second company, which succeeded. The first "failure" became the foundation of her resilience.

Practical Reframing Techniques for Resilience

1. The "What Else Could This Mean?" Method

When adversity strikes, ask: *What other interpretations exist?* For example: instead of "This proves I'm not capable," try "This shows me where I need to grow."

2. The Temporal Reframe

Ask: *How will I see this in one year? Five years?* This shifts perspective, reducing the weight of the present moment.

3. From "Why Me?" to "What Now?"

Replace the disempowering question *"Why me?"* with the empowering *"What now?"* This moves focus from self-pity to constructive action.

4. Stress as Preparation

Reframe stressful moments as training for bigger challenges ahead. For example, public speaking nerves become practice for future leadership roles.

5. Silver-Lining Search

Ask: *Is there any benefit hidden here?* Even painful experiences often carry lessons, growth, or empathy.

6. Humor as Reframe

Finding humor in difficulty lightens perspective. Humor does not erase pain but reduces its weight.

Real-World Example: The Student's Academic Setback

Daniel failed an important exam. His initial frame was despair: *"I'm not smart enough."* With guidance, he reframed: *"This failure shows I need new study strategies."* He sought help, improved methods, and passed the retake. The resilience gained through reframing carried into future challenges.

The Role of Community in Reframing

Resilience is not built alone. Conversations with supportive others provide alternative frames. A trusted friend can help reframe despair into possibility. Communities normalize struggle and remind us we are not alone, which itself reframes adversity from isolation to shared humanity.

Barriers to Reframing

1. **Attachment to Old Stories**: People cling to narratives of victimhood or inadequacy.
2. **Intensity of Emotion**: Strong emotions initially block reframing. Pausing and regulating emotions first makes reframing easier.
3. **Cultural Conditioning**: Some environments reinforce negative frames ("Failure means shame").

Awareness of these barriers allows us to overcome them with patience and practice.

Real-World Example: The Athlete's Injury

Lina, a marathon runner, suffered a severe knee injury that ended her competitive career. At first, she framed it as the end of her identity. Through therapy, she reframed: *"This injury allows me to mentor younger athletes and focus on wellness."* Her career shifted, but her passion for athletics continued. Resilience came from reframing loss into transformation.

The Deeper Lesson: Resilience as a Mental Choice

Life will always present hardships. Resilience does not eliminate pain but transforms it. By reframing, we choose growth over despair, agency over helplessness, hope over fear.

The freedom of resilience lies in realizing: while we cannot always choose events, we can always choose perspective.

Takeaway: Reframe to Rise

Resilience is not innate toughness but mental flexibility. By reframing failure as feedback, rejection as redirection, uncertainty as possibility, and stress as preparation, we transform adversity into growth.

The mind becomes free not when life is easy, but when perspective is strong. Reframing builds that strength. With each reframe, resilience grows, and with resilience, we gain the freedom to face life's storms with clarity and courage.

CHAPTER 8

Meditation, Mindfulness & Stillness

What Mindfulness Really Means (Beyond Hype)

In the past two decades, mindfulness has gone from a quiet contemplative practice to a cultural phenomenon. Corporations offer mindfulness workshops, apps promise instant calm, and social media is filled with quotes about "being present." Yet amid this popularity, the meaning of mindfulness has often been diluted, reduced to buzzwords or quick-fix techniques.

To understand how mindfulness truly supports mental freedom, we must go beyond the hype. At its essence, mindfulness is not about exotic rituals, emptying the mind, or escaping reality. It is the simple but profound practice of paying attention—deliberately, nonjudgmentally, and with curiosity—to the present moment. This practice, while deceptively simple, has transformative effects on clarity, focus, and emotional well-being.

Defining Mindfulness Clearly

Jon Kabat-Zinn, founder of Mindfulness-Based Stress Reduction (MBSR), defines mindfulness as "paying attention in a particular way: on purpose, in the present moment, and nonjudgmentally." Three elements stand out:

1. **Intentional Attention**: Choosing to direct awareness rather than drifting in autopilot.
2. **Present Focus**: Anchoring in what is happening here and now rather than past regrets or future worries.
3. **Nonjudgment**: Observing thoughts, feelings, and sensations without labeling them as good or bad.

Mindfulness is not about suppressing thoughts or striving for constant calm. It is about seeing clearly whatever arises—stress, joy, distraction, or peace.

Why Mindfulness Matters for Mental Freedom

The human mind spends much of its time wandering. A Harvard study found that people's minds wander nearly 47% of the time—and that wandering is often linked to unhappiness. We replay the past, anticipate the future, or escape into distraction. While useful in moderation, unchecked mind-wandering fuels overthinking, anxiety, and stress.

Mindfulness counters this by gently bringing attention back to the present. In doing so, it:

- Reduces overthinking by breaking thought loops.
- Calms emotional reactivity by observing instead of fusing with feelings.
- Enhances focus by training attention.
- Builds acceptance, reducing inner resistance to reality.

The Neuroscience of Mindfulness

Brain imaging studies reveal that mindfulness changes the brain:

- It reduces activity in the **default mode network (DMN)**, the system linked to mind-wandering and rumination.
- It increases gray matter density in areas related to attention, memory, and emotion regulation.
- It lowers amygdala reactivity, reducing stress responses.

In practical terms, mindfulness rewires the brain to spend less time looping and more time anchored in clarity.

Common Misconceptions About Mindfulness

1. **Myth: Mindfulness Means Emptying the Mind**
   Reality: The mind will always produce thoughts. Mindfulness is about noticing them without getting lost.

2. **Myth: Mindfulness Requires Hours of Meditation**
   Reality: Even brief moments of mindful awareness can shift perspective. Consistency matters more than duration.
3. **Myth: Mindfulness Is About Relaxation**
   Reality: Mindfulness sometimes brings discomfort by exposing hidden emotions. The goal is awareness, not escape.
4. **Myth: Mindfulness Is a Religious Practice**
   Reality: While rooted in contemplative traditions, mindfulness itself is secular and accessible to anyone.

Real-World Case Study: The Distracted Student

Maya, a university student, struggled with constant distractions and anxiety. She believed mindfulness meant "not thinking," which felt impossible. A mentor reframed it: mindfulness is simply noticing distractions and returning gently to the present. With five minutes daily of mindful breathing, Maya's focus improved. She realized mindfulness was not about perfection but practice.

Everyday Mindfulness: Beyond Formal Meditation

Mindfulness does not require a cushion or incense. It can be practiced in daily activities:

- Eating: Savoring the taste and texture of each bite.
- Walking: Feeling the ground beneath your feet and the rhythm of your steps.
- Listening: Giving full attention to someone's words without planning your response.
- Waiting: Using moments in line or traffic as cues to breathe and notice the present.

These practices weave mindfulness into ordinary life, making it a way of being rather than a separate activity.

The Role of Nonjudgment

One of the most powerful aspects of mindfulness is nonjudgment. Many people suffer not only from experiences but from judgments about those experiences: *"I shouldn't feel this way."* Mindfulness teaches us to notice without condemning. For example:

- Instead of "I am anxious and weak," shift to "I notice anxiety is present."
  This subtle shift reduces shame and creates space for acceptance and change.

Practical Steps to Begin Mindfulness

1. **Start Small**: Begin with one to three minutes of mindful breathing daily.
2. **Anchor Attention**: Focus on the breath, body sensations, or sounds.
3. **Expect Distractions**: Notice when the mind wanders, and gently return.
4. **Bring Curiosity**: Treat each moment as new, even familiar ones.
5. **Integrate into Routines**: Link mindfulness to daily habits like brushing teeth or drinking tea.

Real-World Example: The Busy Executive

Daniel, a senior executive, dismissed mindfulness as impractical. Constant deadlines left him stressed. At a leadership retreat, he practiced three minutes of mindful breathing before meetings. The result surprised him: he spoke more clearly, felt calmer, and noticed better decision-making. Mindfulness, he realized, was not time lost but time regained.

The Deeper Lesson: Presence Is Freedom

Much of mental suffering comes from living anywhere but the present—rehashing past mistakes, worrying about future outcomes, or numbing through distractions. Mindfulness restores presence. In presence, clarity arises, emotions stabilize, and peace becomes possible even amid difficulty.

Mindfulness is not hype, though it has been hyped. At its essence, it is a practice as old as humanity: noticing life as it unfolds, without running from it or clinging to it.

Takeaway: Awareness Is Liberation

Mindfulness is not about emptying the mind or chasing bliss. It is about seeing clearly. By paying attention intentionally, nonjudgmentally, and in the present, we loosen the grip of overthinking and emotional reactivity.

The power of mindfulness lies in its simplicity. With each breath noticed, each distraction observed, each moment embraced, we reclaim mental freedom—not by changing life, but by changing how we meet it.

Simple 5-Minute Mindfulness Exercises

One of the greatest misconceptions about mindfulness is that it requires long hours of silent meditation in retreat-like settings. While extended practice has its place, most people can begin reaping the benefits of mindfulness in just a few minutes each day. Short, intentional exercises—when practiced consistently—rewire attention, calm the nervous system, and reduce the grip of overthinking.

These micro-practices fit easily into modern schedules, making mindfulness accessible not as an abstract concept but as a lived habit. With only five minutes, we can shift from distraction to clarity, from stress to presence.

Why Short Mindfulness Practices Work

The brain responds quickly to intentional attention. Studies show even brief sessions of mindfulness lower cortisol, reduce mind-wandering, and increase emotional regulation. Just as physical exercise builds strength through repetition, short daily mindfulness practices build mental resilience over time.

Importantly, five-minute exercises are not about achieving perfection. The mind will wander. Distractions will arise. The goal is simply to notice and return, strengthening awareness with each repetition.

Preparing for Practice

Before exploring specific exercises, a few principles enhance effectiveness:

- **Environment**: Choose a quiet spot if possible, but don't wait for perfect silence. Life's background noise can be part of the practice.
- **Posture**: Sit upright but relaxed, feet grounded. You may also practice standing or lying down.
- **Attitude**: Approach with curiosity rather than expectation. Each session is practice, not performance.
- **Consistency**: Five minutes daily is more impactful than an hour occasionally.

Exercise 1: The Five-Breath Reset

Purpose: Instant grounding in the present.

Practice:

1. Sit comfortably.
2. Inhale slowly for a count of four.
3. Hold gently for a count of two.
4. Exhale for a count of six.
5. Repeat for five breaths, noticing the rhythm.

Application: Use anytime stress spikes—before meetings, during conflict, or when overthinking spirals.

Benefit: Calms the nervous system and creates immediate clarity.

Exercise 2: Body Scan in Miniature

Purpose: Release tension and increase bodily awareness.

Practice:

1. Close your eyes.
2. Bring attention to the crown of your head.
3. Slowly move attention downward—forehead, jaw, shoulders, chest, arms, stomach, legs, feet.
4. At each spot, notice sensations without judgment.

Application: Perfect for short breaks at work or before bed.

Benefit: Reduces physical tension, reconnects body and mind.

Exercise 3: The 5-4-3-2-1 Grounding

Purpose: Anchor in the present through the senses.

Practice: Notice:

- 5 things you can see.
- 4 things you can touch.
- 3 things you can hear.
- 2 things you can smell.
- 1 thing you can taste.

Application: Use when overwhelmed or anxious.

Benefit: Redirects attention from racing thoughts to the stability of the present.

Exercise 4: Thought Watching

Purpose: Reduce attachment to thoughts.

Practice:

1. Sit quietly and notice thoughts as they arise.
2. Imagine each thought as a cloud passing in the sky or a leaf floating down a stream.
3. Instead of engaging, observe and let go.

Application: Use during moments of overthinking.

Benefit: Weakens the grip of looping thoughts, fostering detachment.

Exercise 5: Gratitude in Five Minutes

Purpose: Shift focus from scarcity to abundance.

Practice:

1. Write down three things you feel grateful for right now.
2. For each, pause and feel the sense of gratitude in your body.
3. Breathe deeply into that feeling.

Application: Morning or evening routine.

Benefit: Enhances positive emotion and reduces stress by reframing perspective.

Exercise 6: The Mindful Sip

Purpose: Bring mindfulness into daily habits.

Practice:

1. Hold a cup of tea, coffee, or water.
2. Notice its temperature, texture, and scent.
3. Take one slow sip, focusing entirely on taste and sensation.
4. Continue drinking with full attention for a few minutes.

Application: Fits seamlessly into morning routines.

Benefit: Transforms ordinary actions into mindfulness practice.

Exercise 7: Listening With Full Attention

Purpose: Improve connection and reduce mental chatter.

Practice:

1. In a conversation, focus fully on the speaker.

2. Notice tone, words, and body language.
3. Resist planning your reply—simply listen.

Application: Use in meetings, friendships, or family interactions.

Benefit: Deepens relationships and reduces mental noise.

Exercise 8: The Mini Walking Meditation

Purpose: Combine movement with awareness.

Practice:

1. Walk slowly in a quiet space.
2. Notice the sensation of each step—the heel touching, the shift of weight, the lift of the foot.
3. Sync breath with steps if helpful.

Application: Ideal during short breaks or commuting.

Benefit: Grounds awareness in movement, reduces stress without needing stillness.

Real-World Case Study: The Overwhelmed Parent

Laura, a mother of two, felt she had no time for mindfulness. A coach suggested five-minute practices. She began using the five-breath reset in the car before picking up her children. This small pause shifted her from stress to presence, improving her patience and connection. She realized mindfulness did not require extra hours—only intention.

Overcoming Obstacles in Short Practices

1. **Restlessness**: The mind may resist slowing down. Reframe restlessness as part of practice, not failure.
2. **Distraction**: Noise or interruptions happen. Notice them, then return.
3. **Perfectionism**: There is no "perfect" mindfulness. The effort itself is success.

Integrating Five-Minute Practices Into Life

- Morning: Start the day with gratitude journaling or breath reset.
- Workday: Pause with a body scan between tasks.
- Evening: Reflect with the 5-4-3-2-1 grounding before sleep.
- Transitions: Use mindful sipping or walking during commutes.

Consistency transforms these moments into anchors of clarity throughout the day.

The Deeper Lesson: Presence Is Built in Minutes

Mindfulness is not a rare state achieved only in monasteries. It is available in minutes, woven into the fabric of daily life. Short practices build resilience, reduce stress, and shift habits of overthinking. They remind us that clarity is always a breath, a pause, or a sip away.

Takeaway: Five Minutes Can Change the Day

Simple mindfulness exercises—breath resets, body scans, sensory grounding, gratitude reflections, mindful sipping, attentive listening, and walking meditations—create powerful shifts in just minutes.

The practice is not about escaping life but entering it more fully. With five minutes of attention, we trade distraction for presence, anxiety for clarity, and busyness for freedom.

Breathwork as a Reset Button

The breath is the most constant rhythm of human life, yet it is often the most overlooked. From birth to death, breath sustains us, yet we rarely pay attention to it. Unlike heartbeat or digestion, breath is unique: it happens automatically, but we can also consciously control it. This makes breathing one of the most powerful tools for regulating the mind and body.

Breathwork—intentional use of breathing patterns—is a direct way to reset mental state. In moments of stress, overwhelm, or overthinking, breath provides an immediate anchor. With just a few minutes of conscious breathing, the nervous system calms, attention sharpens, and clarity returns.

The Science of Breath and Stress

Breathing is intimately connected to the nervous system.

- **Shallow, rapid breathing** activates the sympathetic nervous system, associated with stress and fight-or-flight responses.
- **Slow, deep breathing** activates the parasympathetic nervous system, associated with rest, recovery, and calm.

Research shows that deliberate breath control can lower cortisol, reduce blood pressure, and quiet the amygdala (the brain's fear center). This explains why breathwork is used in mindfulness, yoga, athletic training, and even therapy for trauma.

Breath as a Bridge Between Body and Mind

The breath links the physical and mental. Stress in the mind creates shallow, tense breathing. Conscious breathing in turn calms the body, signaling safety to the brain. This two-way relationship makes breathwork a reset button: by changing breath, we change both body and thought.

Why Breathwork Helps Overthinking

Overthinking traps the mind in endless loops. Conscious breathing interrupts this cycle by shifting focus from abstract thoughts to concrete sensations. The rhythm of breath brings awareness to the present, creating space from mental noise.

Practical Breathwork Techniques

Different techniques serve different needs—calming anxiety, energizing focus, or balancing emotions.

1. Box Breathing (4-4-4-4)

Purpose: Calm nerves and stabilize focus.

Practice:

1. Inhale for a count of four.
2. Hold for a count of four.
3. Exhale for a count of four.
4. Hold for a count of four.
5. Repeat for several cycles.

Application: Used by Navy SEALs to maintain calm under pressure.

Benefit: Balances oxygen and carbon dioxide, reduces stress, sharpens focus.

2. 4-7-8 Breathing

Purpose: Deep relaxation and sleep support.

Practice:

1. Inhale through the nose for four counts.
2. Hold for seven counts.
3. Exhale slowly through the mouth for eight counts.
4. Repeat four cycles.

Application: Evening routine or during insomnia.

Benefit: Lowers heart rate, engages parasympathetic system, eases anxiety.

3. Alternate Nostril Breathing (Nadi Shodhana)

Purpose: Balance energy and calm the mind.

Practice:

1. Close right nostril with thumb, inhale left.
2. Close left nostril, exhale right.
3. Inhale right, close, exhale left.
4. Continue alternating.

Application: Morning practice or pre-meeting reset.

Benefit: Balances hemispheres of the brain, clears mental fog.

4. Coherent Breathing (5-5 Rhythm)

Purpose: Maintain calm clarity.

Practice:

1. Inhale for five seconds.
2. Exhale for five seconds.
3. Continue for five minutes.

Application: Daily stress prevention.

Benefit: Synchronizes heart rate and breath, creating heart-brain coherence.

5. Breath Counting

Purpose: Build focus and mindfulness.

Practice:

1. Inhale, exhale, count "one."
2. Continue to ten, then restart.
3. If distracted, return to one without judgment.

Application: Mind-wandering reduction.

Benefit: Strengthens concentration, reveals mental patterns.

6. Energizing Breath (Kapalabhati)

Purpose: Boost energy and alertness.

Practice:

1. Sit upright.
2. Inhale gently.
3. Exhale forcefully through nose, contracting abdomen.

4. Repeat rapidly for 20–30 cycles.

Application: Morning energy or pre-work boost.

Benefit: Increases oxygenation, awakens the mind.

Real-World Case Study: The Stressed Executive

Marcus, an executive, often entered meetings tense and reactive. A coach taught him box breathing. Before each meeting, Marcus spent two minutes practicing. The result: calmer presence, clearer communication, and reduced conflict. Breathwork became his reset button in high-stress environments.

Breathwork and Emotional Regulation

Emotions manifest physically. Anger quickens breath, fear shortens it, sadness deepens it. By shifting breath, we shift emotions:

- To calm anger: slow, deep exhalations.
- To soothe anxiety: rhythmic breathing.
- To lift fatigue: energizing breaths.

Breath becomes not only a reset button but a tool for emotional mastery.

Integrating Breathwork Into Daily Life

- **Morning**: Use energizing breath to awaken.
- **Midday**: Practice box breathing to reset focus.
- **Evening**: Use 4-7-8 breathing for relaxation.
- **Stressful Moments**: Pause for three deep belly breaths before reacting.

Consistency creates a habit where breath becomes the natural first step in stress.

Overcoming Obstacles in Breathwork

1. **Restlessness**: Beginners may feel uncomfortable slowing down. Start with one minute and build gradually.
2. **Distraction**: Thoughts will wander. Notice and return to breath.
3. **Impatience**: Results may feel subtle at first. With practice, effects accumulate.

The Deeper Lesson: Breath as Freedom

The breath is always available, always free, and always in the present moment. It cannot be taken away by circumstance. This makes it the ultimate anchor for mental freedom.

When life feels chaotic, the breath reminds us of choice: we can react unconsciously or reset consciously. Each inhalation is renewal, each exhalation release.

Takeaway: Pause, Breathe, Reset

Breathwork is more than technique—it is a philosophy of presence. By practicing methods like box breathing, 4-7-8, alternate nostril breathing, and coherent breathing, we reclaim agency over stress and overthinking.

Whenever the mind spirals, the breath offers a reset button. A pause, a breath, a reset—and the mind is free again.

Using Visualization to Unlock Mental Peace

The human mind is a storyteller. It constantly creates images, scenarios, and narratives, whether replaying the past, imagining the future, or interpreting the present. This power of imagination can be a source of stress when left unchecked—filling the mind with worries, regrets, or catastrophic "what-ifs." Yet when guided intentionally, imagination becomes a tool for healing, focus, and inner calm.

Visualization, the practice of creating deliberate mental images, is one of the most effective ways to harness imagination for peace. Athletes use it to prepare for competition, surgeons use it to rehearse procedures, and therapists use it to reduce anxiety. For cultivating mental freedom, visualization allows us to quiet loops of worry and replace them with images of calm, strength, and possibility.

The Psychology of Visualization

Visualization works because the brain responds to imagined experiences almost as if they were real. Studies in neuroscience show that imagining an action activates many of the same neural pathways as performing it physically. This means visualizing relaxation, focus, or success can create measurable changes in mood and performance.

In psychology, visualization is linked to **guided imagery**—a therapeutic practice where individuals use mental images to reduce stress and promote healing. The mind-body connection is so strong that imagery can influence heart rate, blood pressure, and even immune response.

Why Visualization Brings Peace

1. **Interrupts Negative Loops**
   By replacing anxious imagery with calming imagery, visualization breaks cycles of overthinking.
2. **Activates the Relaxation Response**
   Imagining peaceful scenes lowers stress hormones and relaxes muscles.
3. **Strengthens Agency**
   Visualization provides a sense of control by showing the mind positive possibilities.

4. **Anchors Attention**
   Focused imagery brings attention to the present, reducing mind-wandering.

Types of Visualization for Mental Peace

1. Peaceful Place Visualization

Purpose: Create calm by imagining a safe, soothing environment.

Practice:

1. Sit comfortably and close your eyes.
2. Imagine a place where you feel completely at peace—beach, forest, mountain, or a childhood room.
3. Engage all senses: What do you see, hear, smell, feel?
4. Stay in this scene for several minutes, breathing slowly.

Benefit: Anchors the nervous system in safety and relaxation.

2. Light Visualization

Purpose: Reduce anxiety and promote healing.

Practice:

1. Imagine a warm light at the crown of your head.
2. With each breath, let the light flow down, filling body with warmth and calm.
3. Picture stress dissolving wherever the light touches.

Benefit: Encourages emotional release and physical relaxation.

3. Goal Visualization

Purpose: Foster confidence and clarity for future challenges.

Practice:

1. Visualize yourself facing an upcoming challenge (presentation, exam, conversation).
2. Imagine yourself calm, prepared, and effective.
3. Picture successful completion, feeling the emotions of confidence and relief.

Benefit: Reduces anticipatory anxiety, increases performance.

4. Breathing With Imagery

Purpose: Combine breathwork and visualization.

Practice:

1. Inhale: Imagine breathing in calmness as blue light.
2. Exhale: Imagine releasing stress as dark smoke.
3. Continue for several minutes.

Benefit: Enhances the effect of breathwork by engaging imagination.

5. Future Self Visualization

Purpose: Inspire growth and resilience.

Practice:

1. Imagine your future self five years from now, having grown through challenges.
2. Visualize their calmness, wisdom, and presence.
3. Ask: *What advice does this future self give me today?*

Benefit: Provides perspective and hope in difficult times.

Real-World Case Study: The Anxious Speaker

Olivia, a marketing professional, dreaded public speaking. Before presentations, she practiced a visualization: standing confidently, breathing steadily, delivering clearly while the audience responded positively. Over time, her anxiety decreased. Visualization rewired her expectations, replacing dread with confidence.

The Neuroscience of Guided Imagery

Studies using fMRI scans show that visualization of peaceful scenes activates brain regions associated with perception and relaxation, even when no external stimuli are present. Athletes who combine physical practice with visualization improve performance more than those who practice physically alone. This demonstrates visualization's capacity to shape both mind and body.

How to Practice Visualization Effectively

1. **Set the Scene**: Choose a quiet moment. Close eyes, relax body.
2. **Engage the Senses**: Use sight, sound, touch, smell, and even taste for vividness.
3. **Anchor With Breath**: Sync imagery with slow breathing for depth.
4. **Repeat Regularly**: Consistency strengthens neural pathways.
5. **Personalize**: Choose imagery that feels natural and meaningful to you.

Real-World Example: The Healing Visualization

After surgery, Jacob struggled with anxiety about recovery. A therapist guided him to visualize his body healing—cells repairing, energy returning. This daily practice reduced his stress and improved sleep. While not a substitute for medicine, visualization complemented his recovery by calming his mind.

Obstacles and Misconceptions

- **"I can't visualize clearly."** Visualization is not about perfect images; even vague impressions are effective.
- **"It's just imagination."** Imagination is powerful; the brain often cannot distinguish vividly imagined events from reality.
- **"It takes too much time."** Even two to five minutes can bring calm.

Everyday Applications of Visualization

- Before stressful events (interviews, exams, conversations).
- During transitions (waking up, commuting, winding down).
- As part of mindfulness routines (combined with breathwork or meditation).

The Deeper Lesson: Imagination as Liberation

Uncontrolled, imagination enslaves us to fear and worry. Directed, imagination liberates us into peace and clarity. Visualization is not fantasy but practice—training the mind to choose empowering imagery over destructive loops.

The gift of visualization is realizing that inner peace is not only found in outer circumstances. It can be cultivated from within, by guiding the mind's natural storytelling toward calm and strength.

Takeaway: See Peace to Feel Peace

Visualization transforms the mind's greatest liability—its tendency to wander—into its greatest asset. By imagining peaceful scenes, light, growth, and successful outcomes, we train the nervous system to respond with calm instead of chaos.

The key is not to escape reality but to reshape how we meet it. When we see peace in the mind, we feel peace in the body—and we carry that peace into the world.

How Stillness Fuels Productivity

In modern culture, productivity is often equated with constant motion—long hours, packed schedules, and relentless activity. Stillness, by contrast, is seen as idleness or laziness, something that slows progress. Yet neuroscience, psychology, and the lived experience of high performers tell a different story: stillness is not the opposite of productivity but its foundation.

Far from being wasted time, stillness restores attention, resets the nervous system, and fosters creativity. It provides the clarity needed to distinguish what truly matters from mere busyness. In a distracted world, learning to embrace stillness may be the most powerful productivity strategy available.

The Myth of Constant Motion

The modern economy rewards speed. We multitask, check notifications compulsively, and fill every gap in the day with activity. Yet studies consistently show that productivity does not rise with longer hours or busier schedules. Instead, it declines: attention fragments, errors increase, and creativity plummets.

Busyness is not the same as effectiveness. In fact, busyness without reflection often creates work that must later be redone. Stillness breaks this cycle by restoring the mind's capacity for depth and precision.

The Science of Stillness and Focus

1. **Attention Restoration Theory**
   Psychologists Stephen and Rachel Kaplan developed this theory, showing that exposure to natural stillness—quiet parks, forests, oceans—restores attention by allowing the brain to rest from directed focus. Even short breaks in still environments recharge concentration.

2. **Default Mode Network (DMN)**
   When the mind is still, the DMN activates. This network supports self-reflection, memory consolidation, and creative insight. Stillness is where the brain connects disparate ideas into new solutions.
3. **Stress Recovery**
   Stillness activates the parasympathetic nervous system, lowering cortisol and heart rate. Reduced stress improves decision-making and emotional regulation—key elements of sustained productivity.

Real-World Case Study: The Overworked Engineer

Raj, a software engineer, prided himself on working ten-hour days without breaks. His productivity, however, was declining. At his manager's suggestion, he began taking short stillness breaks: closing his laptop, breathing deeply, and gazing out the window for five minutes each hour. To his surprise, his output improved. Bugs decreased, and creative solutions emerged more easily. Stillness gave him back efficiency.

How Stillness Fuels Different Aspects of Productivity

1. Clarity of Priorities

Stillness allows reflection: *What matters most? What is noise?* Without pauses, people confuse urgent with important, filling days with tasks that do not serve long-term goals.

2. Enhanced Creativity

Breakthroughs rarely happen in chaos. They arise in quiet—while showering, walking, or sitting still. Stillness allows ideas to connect beneath the surface.

3. Emotional Regulation

Stress narrows focus to immediate threats. Stillness widens perspective, reducing reactivity and allowing measured decisions.

4. Sustainable Energy

Continuous work drains energy. Stillness restores it, preventing burnout and maintaining steady performance.

Practical Ways to Practice Stillness for Productivity

1. Micro-Pauses

Take one to three minutes of stillness between tasks. Close eyes, breathe, and reset. These micro-pauses reduce mental residue from one task before starting the next.

2. Morning Stillness

Begin the day with five minutes of stillness before checking devices. This anchors attention before the flood of input.

3. Midday Reset

Schedule a short stillness practice—breathing, meditation, or quiet walking—during lunch. This prevents the afternoon slump.

4. Evening Reflection

Use stillness before bed to review the day and release tension. A quiet journal entry or mindful breathing clears the mind for restful sleep.

5. Tech-Free Spaces

Designate areas of stillness—bedrooms, dining tables, parks—where devices are absent. These spaces preserve uninterrupted presence.

Techniques for Cultivating Stillness

- **Mindful Breathing**: Focus on slow, steady inhales and exhales.
- **Nature Immersion**: Spend time in quiet natural settings.
- **Silent Sitting**: Sit without agenda, allowing thoughts to come and go.
- **Visualization**: Imagine a peaceful scene to anchor stillness.
- **Gratitude Pause**: Reflect quietly on three things you value.

Real-World Example: The Creative Breakthrough

A novelist struggled with writer's block, forcing herself to sit at her desk for hours. Eventually, she began taking twenty-minute stillness walks each morning without her phone. Within weeks, ideas flowed again. The stillness unlocked creativity that strain had blocked.

Overcoming Resistance to Stillness

Many resist stillness because:

- **Guilt**: Believing productivity requires constant action.
- **Restlessness**: Unused to silence, the mind resists slowing down.
- **Fear of Thoughts**: Stillness surfaces emotions or worries previously avoided.

These challenges are normal. With practice, the discomfort eases, revealing stillness as strength rather than weakness.

Integrating Stillness Into Work Culture

Progressive organizations are recognizing stillness as a productivity tool. Google and Intel have mindfulness programs. Some companies encourage "no-meeting mornings" or quiet rooms. Far from reducing output, these practices improve innovation and morale.

The Deeper Lesson: Productivity Is About Depth, Not Speed

True productivity is not doing more but doing what matters with clarity. Stillness fuels this by quieting noise, restoring attention, and allowing reflection. In a world obsessed with acceleration, stillness is rebellion—and wisdom.

Takeaway: Pause to Progress

Stillness is not wasted time; it is the foundation of effectiveness. By integrating micro-pauses, morning quiet, nature breaks, and evening reflection, we harness stillness as fuel for productivity.

The paradox is clear: when we stop, we move forward more wisely. Stillness transforms busyness into meaningful progress, giving us not just efficiency but freedom.

CHAPTER 9

Reprogramming Beliefs & Identity

The Stories You Tell Yourself

Every person carries an invisible narrator inside their mind. This narrator tells stories about who they are, what they are capable of, and how the world works. These internal stories are not always conscious, but they shape nearly every decision, reaction, and belief. They are the scripts of identity, and whether empowering or limiting, they define the boundaries of mental freedom.

Some stories uplift: *"I can learn from mistakes," "I am worthy of love," "Challenges are opportunities."* Others confine: *"I'll never be good enough," "People always let me down," "I'm not smart enough to succeed."* These narratives are not facts—they are interpretations. Yet because the brain clings to stories to make sense of life, they often feel absolute.

To reprogram beliefs and identity, the first step is recognizing the stories we tell ourselves. Only then can we rewrite them into narratives that align with growth, freedom, and resilience.

Why Humans Live Through Stories

Humans are storytelling beings. Neuroscience shows that the brain is wired for narrative: we process experiences as plots with causes, consequences, and meaning. This is why people remember stories more easily than facts and why we naturally explain our lives as unfolding narratives.

Stories help us make sense of chaos. When events occur, the mind asks: *What does this mean about me? What does this mean about the world?* The answers form our personal myths. But not all myths are liberating. Some become cages, narrowing what we believe possible.

The Power of Internal Narratives

The stories you tell yourself act as:

1. **Identity Shapers**
   They determine how you see yourself. *"I'm the type of person who always fails"* creates a self-fulfilling prophecy.
2. **Decision Filters**
   They influence choices. Someone with the story *"I'm unlucky"* may avoid opportunities, assuming they won't work out.
3. **Emotional Amplifiers**
   They magnify feelings. A rejection can be framed as evidence of *"I'm unlovable"* or *"This wasn't the right fit."* The story changes the emotional impact.
4. **Relationship Scripts**
   They affect how you connect. If your story is *"People can't be trusted,"* you will struggle with intimacy and collaboration.

Real-World Case Study: The Student With a Story of Failure

Daniel grew up hearing he wasn't "the smart one" in the family. He internalized the story *"I'm not intelligent."* In school, he avoided advanced classes, believing he'd fail. Later, a mentor challenged this story, encouraging him to see effort as intelligence. Reframing his story, Daniel began excelling academically. His capability was never absent; his story had held him back.

Common Types of Limiting Stories

1. **The Fixed Identity Story**: *"This is just who I am. I can't change."*
2. **The Scarcity Story**: *"There's never enough for me—time, love, opportunity."*

3. **The Victim Story**: *"Life always happens to me; I have no control."*
4. **The Comparison Story**: *"Others are always better than me."*
5. **The Inherited Story**: Beliefs passed from family or culture, such as *"Our kind of people don't succeed."*

These stories persist because the brain seeks confirmation bias, noticing evidence that supports them while ignoring contradictions.

Why Stories Feel So Real

Stories feel true because they are reinforced by emotion and repetition. Each time a thought repeats, neural pathways strengthen. Over time, the story becomes automatic. For example, telling yourself *"I'm bad at relationships"* after a breakup cements the belief, making the next relationship harder.

But just as repetition entrenches limiting stories, repetition can rewire empowering ones.

Techniques to Identify Your Stories

1. Listen to Your Self-Talk

Notice recurring phrases: *"I can't,"* *"I always,"* *"I never."* These often reveal core stories.

2. Write "I Am" Statements

Fill in blanks: *"I am… I am not…"* The answers expose identity narratives.

3. Trace Back to Origin

Ask: *Where did this story begin? Was it mine or someone else's?* Many limiting beliefs are inherited rather than chosen.

4. Notice Emotional Reactions

Strong emotions often point to stories being activated. If criticism feels unbearable, perhaps your story is *"I'm worthless."*

Rewriting Stories: The Reframe

Identifying limiting stories is only step one. The deeper work is rewriting them.

1. Question the Evidence

Is this story universally true, or is it based on selective memories? Challenge its foundation.

2. Replace Absolutes With Growth Language

Shift *"I always fail"* to *"Sometimes I struggle, but I can learn and improve."*

3. Use Alternative Narratives

Choose stories that empower:

- From victimhood: *"Life happens to me"* → *"Life challenges me to grow."*
- From scarcity: *"There isn't enough"* → *"Opportunities are abundant if I stay open."*
- From inadequacy: *"I'm not enough"* → *"I am evolving and learning every day."*

4. Anchor in Evidence of Change

Recall times you succeeded, learned, or overcame. Use these as counterproof against limiting stories.

5. Repeat and Reinforce

New stories must be repeated consistently. Journaling, affirmations, or guided visualization strengthen new neural pathways.

Real-World Example: The Entrepreneur's Shift

Leah, an aspiring entrepreneur, carried the story *"I'm not business-minded."* After a failed first venture, she nearly gave up. Through coaching, she reframed: *"I'm still learning the skills of business."* With persistence, she launched a successful online store. Changing the story changed her future.

The Role of Self-Compassion in Story Change

Many resist rewriting stories because of shame: *"If I've believed this, something must be wrong with me."* But self-compassion reframes the process: stories are natural survival tools, not moral flaws. They were created to protect you at one point. Now, they can be updated.

How Stories Shape Identity

Identity is not fixed but fluid, shaped by the stories we believe. By rewriting stories, we do not deny the past—we reinterpret it. Instead of being "the person who always fails," we become "the person who persists and learns." Identity evolves with narrative.

The Deeper Lesson: Freedom Is Narrative Choice

Mental freedom does not require erasing all stories but choosing them consciously. Life will always involve narrative; the key is authorship. Are you the passive character repeating inherited scripts, or the author rewriting them toward growth?

Takeaway: Rewrite the Script

The stories you tell yourself are not facts but interpretations. By identifying limiting narratives and consciously reframing them, you reclaim authorship of identity.

Every new story becomes a doorway to freedom. The question is not whether you have stories but whether you choose them—or let them choose you.

Affirmations vs. Evidence: What Actually Works

Self-help advice often promotes affirmations—positive statements repeated daily, such as *"I am confident,"* *"I am successful,"* or *"I am worthy."* Advocates claim that affirmations reshape beliefs and attract desired outcomes. Yet many people try affirmations only to find them hollow or ineffective. They repeat words that feel untrue, leaving them discouraged or even more doubtful than before.

Why do affirmations work for some but fail for others? The answer lies in understanding the psychology of belief. While affirmations can be helpful, they are not magic spells. True belief change requires more than repeating words—it requires evidence.

The Psychology of Belief Change

Beliefs are built from repeated experiences and reinforced through evidence. When you touch fire and get burned, your brain encodes the belief *"fire is dangerous."* When you consistently succeed at learning, your brain encodes the belief *"I am capable."* Beliefs are essentially conclusions drawn from patterns of experience.

This is why affirmations often fail: repeating *"I am successful"* without supportive evidence creates internal conflict. The brain resists, arguing: *"But that's not true."* Instead of empowerment, affirmations trigger cognitive dissonance—mental discomfort from holding contradictory beliefs.

Why Affirmations Alone Can Backfire

1. **Mismatch With Current Beliefs**
   If someone deeply believes *"I'm not good enough,"* repeating *"I am amazing"* may feel like lying.
2. **Triggering Inner Critic**
   Affirmations can amplify self-doubt if the mind immediately counters: *"No, you're not."*
3. **Lack of Action**
   Words without behavior change remain empty. Affirmations without aligned action do not shift identity.

The Role of Evidence in Belief Formation

The brain craves congruence. It aligns beliefs with lived evidence. For example:

- If you affirm *"I am disciplined"* but consistently procrastinate, the brain defaults to evidence of procrastination.
- If you take small disciplined actions—waking up on time, finishing tasks—the brain begins to accept the belief, reinforced by evidence.

Thus, evidence is the bridge between words and identity.

Affirmations That Work: Evidence-Linked

Affirmations become powerful when paired with actions that generate confirming evidence. For example:

- Instead of *"I am confident,"* try: *"I am learning to act with confidence by practicing speaking up."*

- Instead of *"I am successful,"* try: *"I am building success step by step through today's efforts."*

These affirmations are believable because they acknowledge process and invite action.

Real-World Case Study: The Public Speaker

Maria struggled with stage fright. She tried affirmations like *"I am a confident speaker,"* but felt like a fraud. Her coach shifted her focus: *"I am becoming more confident each time I practice."* Maria paired this with regular speaking practice. Over time, evidence accumulated, and her belief shifted naturally. Affirmations worked because they were grounded in reality.

Strategies for Belief Change

1. Start With Evidence-Based Affirmations

Use statements that reflect growth rather than fixed outcomes:

- "I am learning…"
- "I am practicing…"
- "I am becoming…"

These align with truth and reduce internal resistance.

2. Collect Small Wins

Document small actions that support new beliefs. For example, if building the belief *"I am disciplined,"* write down each time you complete a task. Over time, the list becomes evidence.

3. Reframe Past Evidence

Look for past experiences that support your new belief but were overlooked. For instance, if you believe *"I always fail,"* recall times you succeeded, however small.

4. Combine Affirmations With Action

Each affirmation should link to behavior: *"I am strong because I exercise daily."* Action makes belief tangible.

5. Use Visualization as Evidence

The brain responds to vivid imagination almost like real experience. Visualizing success can serve as mental rehearsal, building a sense of evidence before action.

Real-World Example: The Aspiring Writer

Ethan wanted to believe he was a writer. Repeating *"I am a great author"* felt false. Instead, he affirmed: *"I am a writer because I write every day."* By committing to 20 minutes of writing daily, evidence aligned with words. Over months, his belief solidified—not through empty affirmations but through repeated proof.

Affirmations vs. Cognitive Reframing

Affirmations focus on declaring a belief. Cognitive reframing, by contrast, questions negative beliefs and replaces them with balanced interpretations. For example:

- Negative thought: *"I'm terrible at this."*
- Reframe: *"I'm still learning, and mistakes are part of the process."*

While affirmations plant seeds, reframing clears the soil. Both work best together: challenge the old belief, then affirm the new one with action-based reinforcement.

The Neuroscience of Belief Change

Neuroplasticity—the brain's ability to rewire—explains how affirmations and evidence work together. Each repeated thought strengthens neural pathways. Each aligned action reinforces them further. Over time, old limiting beliefs weaken, and new empowering beliefs take hold.

Practical Daily Framework

1. **Morning Affirmation (Evidence-Based)**
   Choose one believable affirmation linked to a daily action. Example: *"I am building focus by practicing single-tasking today."*
2. **Daily Action**
   Engage in the behavior that supports the belief.
3. **Evening Reflection**
   Record evidence: *"I completed my task without distraction for 30 minutes."*
4. **Weekly Review**
   Look back at collected evidence. This reinforces the belief as reality.

Obstacles in Belief Reprogramming

- **Impatience**: Beliefs shift gradually. Expecting instant transformation leads to discouragement.
- **All-or-Nothing Thinking**: Progress comes in steps, not perfection.
- **Inherited Scripts**: Old family or cultural beliefs may resist change; persistence is required.

Real-World Example: The Fitness Journey

Lily believed *"I'm not athletic."* Affirmations like *"I am fit"* felt untrue. Instead, she began affirming: *"I am becoming stronger with each workout."* Each gym session provided evidence. Over time, her belief shifted from "not athletic" to "disciplined and capable."

The Deeper Lesson: Belief Requires Proof

Words can inspire, but only evidence convinces. Affirmations without action are wishful thinking; affirmations with evidence are identity change. The most powerful identity shifts occur when what you tell yourself and what you do align consistently.

Takeaway: Build Belief With Action

Affirmations alone are fragile. Affirmations supported by evidence are transformative. By choosing growth-based statements, pairing them with aligned actions, and collecting proof, you reprogram beliefs and identity authentically.

Mental freedom is not about chanting empty words. It is about living in a way that proves your new story true, day by day.

Building a Growth Identity Step by Step

Identity is one of the most powerful forces shaping human behavior. More than goals, habits, or even external rewards, the way we see ourselves—our identity—determines the choices we make and the lives we lead. If you believe *"I'm not disciplined,"* you will act accordingly. If you believe *"I'm a resilient person,"* you will persist when challenges arise.

Yet identity is not fixed. It evolves. We are not bound to the labels we inherited or the stories we once believed. Identity is built moment by moment, through actions repeated consistently. This is the essence of a growth identity: rather than seeing yourself as static, you see yourself as evolving, capable of learning, and defined by progress, not perfection.

The Psychology of Identity

Psychologists explain identity as the internalized sense of self—how we answer the question: *"Who am I?"* It is shaped by early experiences, cultural expectations, and personal choices. Over time, identity becomes a self-reinforcing loop:

- Beliefs influence actions.
- Actions provide evidence.
- Evidence strengthens beliefs.

For example: believing *"I'm not athletic"* leads to avoiding exercise, which reinforces the belief. Conversely, believing *"I'm becoming healthier"* encourages small actions, which provide proof and strengthen the new identity.

Why Growth Identity Matters

1. **Resilience**: A growth identity frames setbacks as temporary, not permanent.
2. **Motivation**: Identity-driven behaviors are stronger than willpower. People act in alignment with who they believe they are.
3. **Freedom**: Identity rooted in growth reduces fear of failure, since failure becomes part of learning.

Fixed vs. Growth Identity

- **Fixed Identity**: *"I am this way, and it cannot change."* Creates rigidity, fear of mistakes, and avoidance of challenges.
- **Growth Identity**: *"I can evolve through effort and experience."* Creates flexibility, persistence, and openness.

Real-World Case Study: From "Non-Reader" to Lifelong Learner

Michael told himself for years, *"I'm not a reader."* School experiences reinforced this belief. In his late twenties, he decided to shift. He began with just five minutes of reading daily, telling himself, *"I am becoming a reader."* Each finished book provided evidence. Today, he reads over 30 books a year. The shift was not from zero to expert overnight, but step by step, identity evolved.

How to Build a Growth Identity Step by Step

1. Define the Identity You Want

Ask: *Who do I want to become?* Not *what do I want to achieve,* but *what kind of person would achieve those things?* For example:

- Goal: Run a marathon.
- Identity: *"I am a runner."*

2. Start With Micro-Actions

Identity shifts require evidence, and evidence begins small. Micro-actions prove to the brain that change is possible. Examples:

- If building *"I am disciplined,"* start by making your bed daily.
- If building *"I am healthy,"* start by drinking one glass of water upon waking.

3. Use the Language of Becoming

Replace static labels with dynamic ones:

- From *"I'm disorganized"* → *"I'm learning to organize my life."*
- From *"I'm anxious"* → *"I'm practicing calm."*

This language reduces resistance and makes growth believable.

4. Collect Proof Daily

Each action becomes evidence. Record it in a journal, app, or calendar. Over time, small wins accumulate into powerful proof of identity.

5. Celebrate Progress, Not Perfection

Growth identity thrives on progress. Even imperfect actions reinforce the identity: showing up for a five-minute workout still supports *"I am active."*

6. Align Environment With Identity

Environments reinforce identity. If you want to build *"I am focused,"* create a clutter-free workspace. If you want *"I am healthy,"* stock nutritious food. Surroundings should echo the identity you are building.

7. Anchor in Community

Community reinforces identity. Join groups that embody the traits you want. If building a runner identity, run with a local group. Shared identity amplifies personal commitment.

Real-World Example: The "Healthy Person" Shift

Sara struggled with dieting, labeling herself as *"unhealthy."* Instead of chasing weight loss goals, she reframed: *"I am becoming someone who prioritizes health."* She started walking daily and cooking simple meals. Each action provided evidence. Within a year, she had lost weight and gained energy—not because of rigid goals, but because her identity shifted to align with health.

Barriers to Growth Identity

1. **Old Stories**: Past failures or family labels resurface.
2. **Impatience**: Identity shifts gradually, not instantly.
3. **All-or-Nothing Thinking**: Believing one slip erases progress.

The key is persistence: remind yourself that each action, however small, contributes to the identity you are building.

The Role of Reflection in Identity Growth

Weekly reflection strengthens growth identity. Ask:

- *What actions proved my new identity this week?*
- *Where did I slip into old patterns?*
- *How can I take one step further next week?*

Reflection prevents discouragement and highlights progress often overlooked.

The Neuroscience of Identity Formation

Habits and identity share neural pathways. Each repeated action strengthens synaptic connections. Over time, the brain associates these actions with self-image. This is why consistency, not intensity, matters most in identity change. Small steps repeated daily literally rewire the brain to accept a new self.

The Deeper Lesson: You Are the Architect of Identity

Identity is not discovered—it is constructed. It is not given—it is chosen. Each day, with each action, you vote for the person you are becoming. You are both the author and the character of your story.

The growth identity perspective liberates you from the prison of past labels. You do not have to remain who you once were. You can design, through practice, who you wish to become.

Takeaway: Identity Is Built, Not Found

Beliefs and habits may shift, but identity solidifies them. By defining the person you want to be, starting with micro-actions, using the language of becoming, collecting daily proof, and aligning environment and community, you build a growth identity step by step.

The truth is simple yet powerful: you do not rise to the level of your goals; you fall to the level of your identity. Choose growth, and build it daily.

How Small Wins Rewrite Your Self-Image

When people think about changing themselves, they often imagine dramatic transformations: quitting a bad habit overnight, launching a business in a month, or reinventing their personality in one bold step. But in reality, self-image—how we see ourselves—rarely shifts through grand gestures. Instead, it is rewritten through small wins accumulated over time.

Self-image is not built in a single moment. It is constructed like a mosaic, piece by piece, with each action adding a tile. Every small victory—getting out of bed on time, saying no to an unhealthy impulse, finishing a task—becomes proof. These small wins, repeated consistently, gradually alter the way we view ourselves. And once self-image changes, behavior follows naturally.

The Psychology of Self-Image

Self-image is the mental picture we hold of ourselves: our abilities, worth, and potential. It is not always accurate; many people underestimate themselves because they cling to outdated or negative stories. Yet self-image is powerful, because behavior tends to align with identity. If you believe *"I'm disorganized,"* you act in ways that confirm disorganization. If you believe *"I'm resilient,"* you persist in difficulties.

Psychologists refer to this as **self-consistency theory**: people are motivated to behave in ways consistent with their self-image. Change, therefore, requires rewriting the image, not just forcing new actions.

Why Small Wins Matter

1. **Evidence Over Willpower**
   Small wins provide tangible proof that counters limiting beliefs. Unlike abstract affirmations, they show the brain: *"I can do this."*
2. **Momentum and Motivation**
   Success breeds success. Each small win builds motivation for the next.
3. **Reduces Resistance**
   Large goals trigger fear and overwhelm. Small wins feel achievable, bypassing resistance.
4. **Shifts Identity Gradually**
   Small actions accumulate into identity: doing one push-up daily reinforces *"I am someone who takes care of my health."*

Real-World Case Study: The Non-Exerciser's Shift

Anthony always told himself, *"I'm not athletic."* He avoided gyms, reinforcing his belief. A friend suggested starting with one push-up a day. At first it seemed trivial, but Anthony kept at it. Soon he added two, then five. After months, he joined a local fitness class. His self-image shifted—not because of one grand achievement, but because daily small wins gave him undeniable evidence: *"I am active."*

The Neuroscience of Small Wins

Neuroscience shows that each small accomplishment releases dopamine, the brain's reward chemical. Dopamine not only feels good but motivates repetition. Over time, small wins strengthen neural pathways, creating habits and reshaping self-perception.

This explains why incremental progress feels disproportionately powerful. The brain interprets each small win as evidence of capability, reinforcing identity change at a biological level.

Strategies to Leverage Small Wins

1. Start Ridiculously Small

Choose an action so small it feels impossible to fail. Examples:

- One push-up.
- Writing one sentence.
- Meditating for one minute.

The goal is not intensity but consistency. Small wins bypass the brain's resistance and create momentum.

2. Anchor Small Wins to Identity

Frame each win as identity proof:

- "I meditated for one minute; I am becoming mindful."
- "I wrote one sentence; I am a writer."
- "I saved one dollar; I am financially responsible."

Identity linkage transforms trivial wins into powerful self-image builders.

3. Track and Celebrate Progress

Recording small wins amplifies their effect. Journals, apps, or calendars provide visible proof that reinforces the new self-image. Celebrating even minor victories builds motivation.

4. Compound the Wins

As confidence grows, increase actions gradually. One push-up becomes five, one sentence becomes a paragraph. Small wins naturally expand into larger ones.

5. Focus on Consistency, Not Perfection

Missed days do not erase progress. Self-image rewrites through persistence, not perfection. The key is returning quickly, reinforcing resilience.

Real-World Example: The Writer's Identity

Emma wanted to write a novel but doubted she had discipline. Instead of aiming for chapters, she committed to writing 50 words daily. Within weeks, she had pages. Months later, she completed her first draft. Each day's small win told her: *"I am a writer."* The novel was a byproduct of self-image change.

Barriers to Small Wins

1. **Impatience**: Desire for quick results undermines gradual progress.
2. **Minimization**: Believing small wins don't matter. In reality, they matter most.
3. **Old Labels**: Past self-image resists new evidence.

Overcoming these barriers requires patience and reframing: every win, no matter how small, is rewriting the script.

The Ripple Effect of Small Wins

Small wins rarely stay confined. Success in one area spills into others:

- Starting with five minutes of exercise builds discipline that carries into work.
- Practicing gratitude daily shifts mood, which improves relationships.
- Saving small amounts creates financial confidence, leading to bigger decisions.

This ripple effect accelerates self-image change across life domains.

The Deeper Lesson: Identity Is Earned Through Repetition

Self-image does not change by wishing. It changes by earning new evidence daily. Each small win is a vote for the person you want to be. Over time, votes accumulate into identity, and identity directs behavior automatically.

Small wins are not just progress—they are transformation in disguise.

Takeaway: Proof, Not Perfection

The mind believes what it sees repeated. Small wins provide the repetition of proof that reshapes self-image. By starting small, linking wins to identity, tracking progress, and compounding success, you rewrite who you believe yourself to be.

The shift is subtle but powerful: from *"I want to be this type of person"* to *"I am this type of person."* And once identity changes, growth becomes inevitable.

Future Self-Journaling to Design Freedom

Every person lives in two timelines: the one unfolding moment by moment, and the one they imagine ahead. This imagined future—whether hopeful or fearful—guides decisions in the present. Someone who sees their future self as capable, resilient, and fulfilled makes different choices than someone who sees only struggle and limitation.

Future self-journaling is a practice that deliberately shapes this vision. By writing consistently from the perspective of who you want to become, you create clarity, direction, and alignment between today's actions and tomorrow's self. It is not fantasy; it is identity design. The written word serves as both mirror and map, reflecting current beliefs and charting a new course.

Why the Future Self Matters

Psychologists have long studied the "future self." Research by Hal Hershfield at UCLA shows that people who feel more connected to their future selves make better long-term decisions—saving money, maintaining health, and resisting destructive impulses. When the future self feels like "a stranger," people prioritize short-term gratification. When the future self feels like "a friend," people act with discipline and care.

Future self-journaling strengthens this connection. By repeatedly envisioning and describing the person you are becoming, you dissolve the gap between present and future.

The Power of Writing in Identity Change

Writing externalizes thought. It transforms vague wishes into structured language. Neuroscience shows that writing activates multiple brain regions, strengthening memory and embedding ideas more deeply. When we write about the future self, we are not only imagining—we are rehearsing, reinforcing, and reprogramming.

How Future Self-Journaling Works

1. **Clarifies Vision**
   Writing paints a vivid picture of who you want to be.
2. **Aligns Behavior**
   When you read and write about your future self daily, your present choices naturally align.
3. **Reframes Identity**
   Instead of clinging to past stories, journaling anchors you in possibility.
4. **Creates Evidence Over Time**
   As journals accumulate, you see growth unfold, reinforcing the belief: *"I am becoming this person."*

Real-World Case Study: The Career Shift

Nina, a corporate employee, felt stuck. She began journaling daily from her future self as an entrepreneur: describing her routines, mindset, and interactions. Within months, her actions shifted—she networked, took courses, and launched a side project. Two years later, she transitioned fully. Journaling didn't magically create success, but it aligned her choices with her envisioned identity until it became reality.

Practical Framework for Future Self-Journaling

Step 1: Choose a Timeframe

Decide whether you are writing to your self six months, one year, or five years in the future. Closer timeframes feel actionable; distant ones expand imagination.

Step 2: Write in Present Tense

Describe the future self as if already real: *"I wake up energized. I lead my team with clarity. I prioritize my health."* This conditions the brain to accept the identity.

Step 3: Engage the Senses

Make it vivid. What does your future morning smell like? What does your environment look like? Sensory detail deepens emotional connection.

Step 4: Focus on Qualities, Not Just Outcomes

Instead of only describing external achievements, focus on internal growth: resilience, discipline, peace. Achievements may change, but qualities sustain.

Step 5: Align With Daily Action

Each journaling session should inspire one action you can take today to move toward that future. This grounds vision in reality.

Journaling Prompts for Designing Freedom

1. What does my future self believe that I do not yet believe?
2. How does my future self handle challenges?
3. What daily habits does my future self practice?
4. What relationships surround my future self?
5. If my future self could speak to me today, what advice would they give?

Real-World Example: The Student's Transformation

Aaron, a college student, lacked confidence. He began journaling as his future self—confident, disciplined, and thriving. He described daily habits: studying with focus, exercising, speaking up in class. As he wrote, he began living these habits. His self-image shifted from insecure to capable, step by step. The practice provided both vision and accountability.

Common Obstacles and How to Overcome Them

1. **Feeling Fake**
   At first, journaling as a confident or successful version of yourself may feel unrealistic. Reframe this as rehearsal, not pretending.
2. **Inconsistency**
   Journaling only works with repetition. Commit to short, daily sessions—five minutes is enough.
3. **Perfectionism**
   Some people fear writing the "wrong" future. Remember: your vision can evolve. Journaling is not prediction but design.

The Neuroscience of Visualization Through Writing

Studies show that combining writing with visualization activates both the prefrontal cortex (logic and planning) and the limbic system (emotion). This dual activation makes goals stickier. Writing also slows thought, forcing clarity. The act of scripting your future self repeatedly strengthens the brain's expectation of that identity.

Expanding Future Self-Journaling Into Daily Life

- **Morning Practice**: Begin the day writing from your future self, setting tone and intention.
- **Evening Reflection**: Write one paragraph comparing today's actions with your envisioned self.
- **Weekly Letters**: Write a letter from your future self to your present self, offering advice and encouragement.
- **Vision Journals**: Combine writing with images or symbols that represent your future self.

Real-World Example: The Athlete's Recovery

Lena, an athlete recovering from injury, struggled with hopelessness. She began journaling as her future self—strong, healed, competing again. This vision kept her motivated during rehab. Months later, she not only recovered but returned stronger. Journaling anchored her in possibility when present reality felt bleak.

The Deeper Lesson: Freedom Is Designed, Not Discovered

Mental freedom is not stumbled upon—it is crafted. Future self-journaling shifts focus from past mistakes to future possibilities, from static identity to evolving growth. It reminds us daily: we are not defined by yesterday but by who we choose to become tomorrow.

Takeaway: Write the Future Into Existence

Future self-journaling is more than reflection—it is construction. By writing consistently as your future self, you strengthen connection to possibility, align present choices with long-term vision, and rewrite identity.

The essence is simple: if you want to become someone new, begin by writing as if you already are. Words become actions, actions become evidence, and evidence becomes identity. Through journaling, you design freedom one page at a time.

CHAPTER 10

Living a Free Mind Lifestyle

Designing Your Daily Blueprint

Mental freedom is not created by grand, occasional breakthroughs—it is cultivated through the structure of daily life. A person may attend a retreat, read an inspiring book, or have a profound moment of clarity, but unless those insights are woven into daily rhythms, they fade. Freedom of mind requires not just inspiration but design.

A daily blueprint is the intentional structure you give your time, attention, and energy. Rather than drifting through the day reacting to circumstances, you proactively shape your routines, habits, and environment to support clarity and focus. This blueprint does not have to be rigid or overwhelming. Instead, it acts as a guide, ensuring that your life reflects your priorities rather than noise or distraction.

Why Daily Design Matters

1. **Habits Shape Identity**
   Research by James Clear and Charles Duhigg shows that identity is built through repeated behaviors. If you want a free mind, your daily habits must support that freedom.
2. **Structure Prevents Chaos**
   Without intentional design, life fills with urgency—emails, notifications, demands. A blueprint ensures important priorities are not crowded out.
3. **Consistency Beats Intensity**
   One day of focus cannot outweigh a month of distraction. A blueprint creates sustainable consistency.
4. **Mental Energy Is Finite**
   Decision fatigue drains clarity. A blueprint reduces unnecessary decisions, conserving energy for what matters.

The Components of a Daily Blueprint

1. Morning Rituals: Setting the Tone

How you begin the day shapes how you carry it. Instead of immediately reacting to emails or social media, a morning ritual anchors the mind in clarity.

Examples:

- **Mindful Breathwork**: Three minutes of calm breathing before engaging the world.
- **Gratitude Journal**: Writing three things you appreciate to prime the brain for positivity.
- **Movement**: A walk, stretch, or workout to energize body and mind.
- **Intention Setting**: Asking, *"What matters most today?"*

Case Study: Sarah, a teacher, used to wake up rushing. By adding ten minutes of journaling and breathwork, she began entering her classroom calmer and more present. Her students noticed the difference.

2. Focus Blocks: Protecting Deep Work

Constant multitasking fragments attention. Instead, schedule focus blocks—periods where you work on a single priority without distraction.

Techniques:

- **Pomodoro Method**: 25 minutes of work, 5-minute break.
- **Time Blocking**: Reserving hours for specific tasks.
- **Digital Minimalism**: Turning off notifications during focus periods.

Evidence: Research by Cal Newport shows that deep work—sustained, distraction-free focus—produces the highest-quality results and deepest satisfaction.

3. Mindful Pauses: Resetting the Mind

Even with focus, mental energy depletes. Short pauses act as resets.

- One deep breath before replying to messages.
- A short walk between meetings.
- Five minutes of silence after lunch.

These pauses prevent buildup of stress and keep the mind sharp.

4. Evening Rituals: Closing the Day

Just as mornings set the tone, evenings set closure. Without intentional closure, stress lingers into sleep.

Examples:

- **Reflection Journal**: Writing what went well and what you learned.
- **Digital Sunset**: Turning off devices an hour before bed.
- **Gratitude Reflection**: Noting small wins from the day.

Case Study: Daniel, an executive, struggled with insomnia. By adding a nightly ritual of reading and journaling instead of scrolling his phone, he began sleeping better and waking with more clarity.

Designing Around Priorities

A blueprint must reflect personal values, not just efficiency. Ask:

- What matters most to me—health, relationships, growth, contribution?
- Does my current daily structure reflect this?
- What small changes would bring alignment?

For example: If relationships matter most, but evenings are consumed by work emails, redesigning evenings as family time aligns life with values.

Overcoming Barriers to Daily Design

1. **Perfectionism**: Many abandon routines after small failures. Remember: consistency, not perfection, matters.
2. **Rigid Thinking**: A blueprint is flexible. Adapt to circumstances without abandoning the whole.
3. **Overload**: Start small—one new habit at a time—then build.

The Neuroscience of Daily Structure

Habits are encoded in the basal ganglia, the brain's habit center. Once formed, they require less mental energy, freeing the prefrontal cortex for higher thinking. A blueprint creates a structure where positive habits run on autopilot, reducing stress and decision fatigue.

Practical Steps to Build Your Blueprint

1. **Audit Current Routine**: Track how you spend time for a week. Identify distractions and wasted energy.
2. **Define Keystone Habits**: Choose one or two habits that influence many others (e.g., exercise, sleep, journaling).
3. **Create a Prototype Day**: Write down your ideal daily flow—morning ritual, focus blocks, mindful pauses, evening closure.
4. **Implement Gradually**: Start with one new ritual and expand.
5. **Review Weekly**: Adjust as needed. Your blueprint evolves with your life.

Real-World Example: The Remote Worker

Maya, working from home, felt scattered. Her blueprint:

- Morning: 10 minutes meditation, 30 minutes writing.
- Workday: 2 focus blocks with breaks.
- Afternoon: Walk outside.
- Evening: No work emails after 7 p.m., journal before bed.

Within weeks, her clarity and productivity increased. She felt less reactive and more aligned with her values.

The Deeper Lesson: Freedom Is Designed Daily

Mental freedom is not an abstract idea. It is lived through structure. Each day designed with intention becomes a building block of a free mind. Without design, external demands dictate life. With design, you reclaim authorship.

Takeaway: Live by Blueprint, Not by Default

A daily blueprint is not a cage—it is a map toward clarity. By creating rituals, focus blocks, mindful pauses, and evening closures, you align time with values and energy with purpose.

The truth is simple: if you don't design your day, someone else will. Designing your blueprint is designing your freedom—one day at a time.

How to Maintain Mental Clarity Long-Term

Clarity of mind is not a one-time achievement. It is not like climbing a mountain where you reach the top and stay there forever. It is more like tending a garden—requiring consistent care, pruning distractions, and nourishing focus. Many people experience bursts of mental clarity after meditation, a retreat, or a breakthrough conversation, but soon slip back into old patterns of distraction, overthinking, and stress.

The real challenge is not achieving clarity, but sustaining it. Long-term mental clarity requires systems, habits, and perspectives that protect the mind from being hijacked by chaos. It is a lifestyle, not a momentary state.

Why Mental Clarity Fades

1. **Information Overload**
   We live in an era of constant input—news, messages, advertisements. The brain, overwhelmed by volume, loses clarity.
2. **Unmanaged Stress**
   Chronic stress floods the brain with cortisol, impairing memory and focus.
3. **Lack of Rituals**
   Without consistent practices to reset, clarity dissipates under daily pressures.
4. **Reactive Living**
   When life is lived only in response to external demands, priorities blur and mental space shrinks.

Principles for Sustaining Clarity

1. Protect Mental Energy Like a Resource

Just as physical energy is finite, so is cognitive energy. Each decision, distraction, or worry drains it. Protecting clarity means being intentional about where energy flows.

Strategies:

- Limit decision fatigue with routines (e.g., meal planning, set work hours).
- Use boundaries with technology (no notifications during focus hours).
- Avoid multitasking; single-tasking preserves focus.

2. Build Reset Rituals

Long-term clarity requires frequent resets, just as the body needs rest.

- **Daily resets**: breathing exercises, short walks, meditation.
- **Weekly resets**: journaling, digital detox, nature immersion.
- **Annual resets**: retreats, vacations, or deep reflection periods.

Case Study: Mark, a lawyer, faced constant mental clutter. By scheduling a weekly "clarity walk" without devices, he re-centered himself, reducing overwhelm.

3. Manage Inputs Wisely

Clarity depends as much on what we exclude as on what we include.

- Curate information: follow fewer but higher-quality sources.
- Limit doomscrolling and unnecessary consumption.
- Replace mindless inputs with mindful learning.

Psychology calls this "attentional diet": what we feed the mind shapes clarity.

4. Anchor in Core Values

Values act as a compass. When clear, they simplify choices and prevent confusion. For example, if health is a core value, decisions about late nights or food become easier. Aligning actions with values reduces mental noise.

5. Prioritize Sleep and Recovery

Neuroscience shows that sleep clears toxins from the brain, consolidates memory, and resets emotional balance. Without quality sleep, clarity erodes. Prioritizing rest is not indulgence but necessity.

6. Practice Emotional Regulation

Unregulated emotions cloud clarity. By pausing before reacting, labeling feelings, and reframing perspectives, the mind regains space for rational thought. Long-term clarity depends on resilience, not absence of stress.

Real-World Case Study: The Entrepreneur's Burnout

Lila, a startup founder, burned out after two years of nonstop work. She realized clarity was impossible without sustainability. By introducing morning journaling, weekly device-free Sundays, and strict evening cutoffs, she regained balance. Her business improved, not worsened, because her decisions were clearer.

Systems for Long-Term Clarity

1. Morning Alignment Ritual

Each day begins with a short practice: breathing, journaling, or reviewing priorities. This anchors clarity before external noise enters.

2. Weekly Reflection System

Every week, spend 30 minutes reviewing:

- What drained my clarity?
- What restored it?
- How can I adjust for next week?

This reflection keeps clarity intentional, not accidental.

3. Environmental Design

Environments either protect or pollute clarity.

- Keep workspaces clutter-free.
- Use calming colors and natural light.
- Create device-free zones.

Design spaces that signal focus and peace.

4. Accountability Structures

Clarity weakens in isolation. Having an accountability partner or community reinforces habits. For instance, meditation groups or productivity circles keep practices consistent.

Common Obstacles and How to Overcome Them

1. **Busyness Addiction**
   Some people equate constant motion with productivity.
   Reframe: clarity creates efficiency, busyness creates burnout.
2. **Inconsistency**
   Skipping practices erodes clarity. Solution: tie resets to existing routines (e.g., breathing before meals).
3. **Over-Optimizing**
   Ironically, trying to perfect clarity routines can cause stress. Remember: the goal is simplicity, not complexity.

The Neuroscience of Sustained Clarity

Clarity depends on the **prefrontal cortex**, which manages attention and decision-making. Chronic stress and overload impair it. Practices like mindfulness, rest, and focused work strengthen it over time. Neuroplasticity ensures that repeated clarity practices literally rewire the brain for focus and calm.

Real-World Example: The Student With Scattered Focus

Maya, a graduate student, struggled with constant distraction. She created a system: morning journaling, blocking apps during study, weekly reflections, and a nightly digital sunset. Within months, her focus and grades improved. More importantly, she felt calmer and more in control of her mind.

The Deeper Lesson: Clarity Is Maintenance

Clarity is not a single event but a continuous practice. Like fitness or relationships, it requires maintenance. Small, consistent actions protect long-term focus far better than occasional intensity.

Takeaway: Build Systems, Not Moments

To maintain mental clarity long-term, treat it like a resource. Protect energy, manage inputs, create reset rituals, align with values, and design supportive environments.

The goal is not to eliminate all stress or distraction, but to build systems that restore clarity again and again. With these systems, mental freedom stops being a fleeting state and becomes a sustainable lifestyle.

Community and Environment as Mental Anchors

Mental freedom is often spoken of as an internal pursuit—rewiring beliefs, practicing mindfulness, managing thoughts. While inner work is essential, it cannot exist in isolation. Human beings are profoundly shaped by their surroundings: the people they interact with and the spaces they inhabit. Just as a seed cannot flourish in barren soil, the mind cannot sustain clarity in environments and communities that drain, distract, or distort its energy.

Your community and environment act as **mental anchors**. They either hold you steady in clarity or pull you back into old patterns. If you want long-term freedom of mind, you must design not only your habits but also the social and physical contexts that shape them.

Why Community and Environment Matter

1. **Social Contagion of Behavior**
   Research by Nicholas Christakis and James Fowler shows that behaviors spread through social networks—happiness, habits, even obesity. If your peers practice mindfulness, discipline, and resilience, you are more likely to adopt the same.

2. **Environmental Cues Shape Habits**
   Behavioral scientist B.J. Fogg emphasizes that environment often dictates behavior more than willpower. A cluttered workspace invites distraction; a minimalist one supports focus.
3. **Energy is Contagious**
   Emotions are contagious. Being around constant negativity amplifies stress, while uplifting communities strengthen resilience.

Community as Anchor

1. Supportive Relationships

Surround yourself with people who believe in growth and mental freedom. Supportive relationships offer encouragement, accountability, and perspective.

Case Study: Daniel, trying to quit overthinking, joined a mindfulness group. Weekly sessions gave him tools and accountability. Alone, he struggled; with community, he thrived.

2. Boundaries With Draining Relationships

Not all relationships support freedom. Some reinforce limiting beliefs or thrive on negativity. Mental freedom requires boundaries—not cutting everyone off, but limiting time and emotional investment in draining dynamics.

Practical Step: Identify "amplifiers" (people who lift you) and "diminishers" (people who drain you). Adjust time accordingly.

3. Mentors and Role Models

Seek those ahead on the path. Mentors anchor you by showing what's possible. Even virtual mentors—through books, talks, or courses—can expand your vision of freedom.

4. Giving Back

Community is not just about receiving. Teaching, supporting, or mentoring others reinforces your own clarity. Contribution transforms identity from seeker to sharer.

Environment as Anchor

1. Physical Space

Your environment either invites clarity or chaos.

- **Clutter-Free Spaces**: Reduce visual noise to calm the mind.
- **Nature Elements**: Plants, natural light, or outdoor time reduce stress and restore focus.
- **Dedicated Zones**: Separate areas for work, rest, and reflection help train the brain to associate spaces with states.

Case Study: Maya redesigned her desk: no phone, only essentials, one plant. She reported deeper focus and less stress simply from the shift in environment.

2. Digital Environment

The digital world is as real an environment as the physical one. Left uncurated, it fills with noise. Curating digital space is essential.

- Unfollow accounts that trigger comparison or anxiety.
- Limit notifications to essentials.
- Design device-free zones or times.

3. Rhythms of Environment

Environment also includes time rhythms. The pace of life—commutes, work schedules, community events—affects mental freedom. Adjust rhythms when possible to align with your needs.

How to Redesign Community and Environment

1. **Audit Current Anchors**
   Ask: Who and what in my life support clarity? Who and what drain it?
2. **Strengthen Positive Anchors**
   Spend more time with supportive people, in inspiring spaces, and within healthy routines.
3. **Introduce Micro-Changes**
   Even small shifts matter—moving your phone charger outside the bedroom, attending one supportive community event, or adding a plant to your workspace.
4. **Create Intentional Rituals With Others**
   Shared meals without devices, walking groups, or family gratitude rituals anchor community and environment together.
5. **Design Accountability**
   Pair with a friend for meditation practice or join a group challenge. Shared accountability sustains clarity.

Real-World Example: The Recovery Journey

Lena struggled with anxiety. Living with roommates who partied constantly, she found it impossible to maintain mindfulness. After moving into a quieter space and joining a local meditation circle, her clarity improved dramatically. The shift was not only internal but environmental.

Overcoming Obstacles

1. **Fear of Change**
   Leaving draining environments or relationships can feel difficult. Reframe it: you're not abandoning, you're choosing alignment.
2. **Isolation Risk**
   Seeking freedom does not mean solitude. Balance alone practices with supportive connection.

3. **Environmental Inertia**
   Spaces and communities may resist change. Start small, proving through micro-shifts that clarity is possible.

The Neuroscience of Social and Environmental Influence

The brain contains **mirror neurons**, which replicate behaviors observed in others. This explains why moods and habits spread socially. Similarly, environmental cues trigger automatic behaviors—like reaching for snacks if visible on the counter. By designing community and environment intentionally, you hack these unconscious systems in your favor.

The Deeper Lesson: You Rise or Fall With Context

No matter how strong your willpower, environment and community shape outcomes. Freedom is not only an individual pursuit—it is relational and spatial. To maintain clarity, you must choose surroundings that reflect your values and communities that reinforce your growth.

Takeaway: Design the Anchors Around You

Mental freedom is anchored not only in your thoughts but in your context. By curating relationships, setting boundaries, seeking mentors, redesigning spaces, and managing digital inputs, you build external anchors that stabilize inner freedom.

The truth is simple: your environment and community are either designing you or you are designing them. Choose wisely, and they will hold you steady in clarity, even when life's storms arrive.

Practicing Gratitude and Presence Daily

Mental freedom is not about eliminating every problem in life. It is about learning to live with openness, clarity, and appreciation—even when circumstances are imperfect. Two daily practices are especially powerful for this: **gratitude** and **presence.**

Gratitude shifts the lens through which you see reality. Instead of obsessing over what is missing, you recognize what is already here. Presence anchors you in the now, breaking free from regret about the past or anxiety about the future. Together, they form a foundation for sustained clarity and peace.

Why Gratitude Matters

Gratitude is not just saying "thank you." It is a mindset—a deliberate focus on what is good, valuable, and supportive in life. Psychologists Robert Emmons and Michael McCullough, leading researchers in gratitude, found that regular gratitude practices increase happiness, improve health, and strengthen resilience.

Gratitude rewires the brain. Neuroscience shows that focusing on appreciation activates the brain's reward system, releasing dopamine and serotonin—the same neurotransmitters linked to joy and motivation. Over time, gratitude literally makes the brain more sensitive to noticing positives.

Why Presence Matters

The mind spends much of its time elsewhere—rehashing mistakes, worrying about the future, or numbing with distractions. Harvard researchers Matthew Killingsworth and Daniel Gilbert found that people's minds wander almost 47% of the time—and that wandering is strongly correlated with unhappiness.

Presence interrupts this wandering. When you are fully in the moment—whether eating, walking, or talking—you experience life more vividly and reduce mental noise. Presence does not mean ignoring the future or past; it means not being trapped by them.

The Connection Between Gratitude and Presence

Gratitude and presence reinforce each other. You cannot feel genuine gratitude without being present to what is here. And presence deepens when you notice, with gratitude, the richness of each moment. Together, they anchor the mind in freedom.

Real-World Case Study: The Busy Professional

Amira, a project manager, lived in constant stress, thinking only about unfinished tasks. A coach suggested a daily gratitude journal—writing three things she appreciated each night. At first, it felt forced. Within weeks, however, she noticed a shift: instead of ending the day with anxiety, she ended with calm. Over time, gratitude made her more present during the day, noticing small joys she used to overlook.

Practical Gratitude Practices

1. **Gratitude Journal**
   Write down three things you are grateful for each day. Be specific: instead of "my job," write "my supportive coworker who helped today."
2. **Gratitude Letters**
   Write a letter to someone who influenced your life positively. Whether or not you send it, the act deepens appreciation.
3. **Micro-Gratitude Moments**
   Pause during the day to notice one thing you appreciate— sunlight, a meal, a conversation.
4. **Gratitude Before Challenges**
   Ask: *What hidden opportunity or lesson might I be grateful for here?* This reframes difficulties.

Practical Presence Practices

1. **Mindful Breath**
   Pause to take three conscious breaths, feeling each inhale and exhale.
2. **Single-Tasking**
   Choose one activity to do without distraction—eating without screens, walking without music, listening without planning a reply.
3. **Sensory Grounding**
   Notice what you see, hear, feel, smell, and taste in the present moment.
4. **Presence Reminders**
   Use cues—like phone alarms or sticky notes—to prompt small returns to presence throughout the day.

Real-World Example: The Parent at Dinner

David realized he was physically present at family dinners but mentally elsewhere, thinking about work. He began practicing mindful eating: tasting food slowly, listening fully to conversations. Over weeks, his relationships deepened. Presence turned routine dinners into moments of connection.

Overcoming Obstacles

1. **Skepticism**
   Some dismiss gratitude as naive or presence as unproductive. In reality, both improve resilience and focus, making life more effective.
2. **Busyness**
   People say they lack time, but gratitude and presence take seconds—a pause to breathe, a note of thanks.
3. **Negativity Bias**
   The brain naturally focuses on problems. Consistent practice retrains it to balance negatives with positives.

The Neuroscience of Daily Gratitude and Presence

- Gratitude activates the **ventromedial prefrontal cortex**, linked to emotional regulation and decision-making.
- Presence reduces activity in the **default mode network** (rumination center), calming overthinking.
- Both practices strengthen neural plasticity, making clarity and joy more natural over time.

The Ripple Effect

Gratitude and presence do not only affect the self. They transform relationships and environments.

- A grateful person uplifts others.
- A present listener deepens trust.
- A calm, present leader inspires focus in teams.

Case Study: A company introduced daily "gratitude circles," where employees shared one positive thing. Over months, stress declined and collaboration improved. Presence and gratitude became cultural anchors.

The Deeper Lesson: Freedom Is Found in the Now

Freedom of mind is not somewhere in the future. It is here, in the way you relate to this moment. Gratitude reveals abundance, presence reveals reality. Together, they liberate the mind from chasing what's missing or resisting what is.

Takeaway: Gratitude + Presence = Daily Freedom

Practicing gratitude and presence daily is simple but profound. Gratitude shifts focus from lack to abundance. Presence shifts focus from distraction to reality. Both are accessible anytime, requiring no tools, only intention.

Mental freedom is not about escaping life but engaging it fully. By appreciating what is here and living in the present, you cultivate clarity that endures beyond circumstances.

Passing on Mental Freedom to Others

Mental freedom is deeply personal, but it is never only personal. The clarity, peace, and resilience you cultivate inevitably ripple outward, shaping how others feel and act around you. Just as anxiety can spread through a family, workplace, or friendship circle, so can calm presence and clarity.

Passing on mental freedom is not about preaching or forcing others to change. It is about living in a way that inspires, supports, and anchors those around you. By embodying the practices of presence, gratitude, and resilience, you become a model and a catalyst. In this way, mental freedom multiplies, becoming not only a private achievement but a shared gift.

Why Passing on Mental Freedom Matters

1. **Social Contagion of Emotion**
   Psychological research shows that emotions are contagious. A calm, grounded person influences others' nervous systems, reducing tension and reactivity.
2. **Role Modeling**
   Albert Bandura's social learning theory emphasizes that people learn more by observing behaviors than by listening to advice. Living mental freedom teaches more than words.
3. **Sustainable Change**
   Personal freedom solidifies when shared. Supporting others reinforces your own practices, turning them into lifestyle rather than fleeting habits.
4. **Collective Resilience**
   Communities anchored in presence, gratitude, and compassion navigate challenges with greater strength than individuals alone.

Real-World Case Study: The Calm Leader

Maria, a hospital nurse manager, practiced mindfulness daily. During a crisis, while others panicked, she remained steady, breathing deeply before responding. Her calmness spread to her team, lowering stress levels and improving cooperation. By living her practice, she passed on freedom without a single lecture.

Ways to Pass on Mental Freedom

1. Lead by Example

The most powerful way to influence others is through presence. If you are attentive in conversation, others feel valued. If you practice gratitude aloud, others begin to notice positives.

Practical Step: Instead of saying, *"You should meditate,"* simply pause to breathe calmly in stressful situations. Others may naturally mirror you.

2. Share Tools, Not Rules

Offer practices as invitations rather than obligations. Share what has worked for you—journaling, breathwork, or gratitude rituals—without expectation.

Example: A friend overwhelmed by stress may not want advice, but you can share: *"Something that's helped me is writing three things I'm grateful for at night. It might work for you too."*

3. Create Shared Rituals

Build collective practices in families, friendships, or teams.

- **Family**: Share one gratitude at dinner.
- **Friends**: Begin gatherings with a moment of presence.
- **Workplace**: Start meetings with one deep breath.

These rituals anchor groups in freedom without demanding individual discipline.

4. Listen With Presence

One of the greatest gifts is being fully present when others speak. Listening without judgment or distraction models clarity and creates space for others' freedom.

Case Study: James, a teacher, made a practice of giving students his full attention. Over time, they mirrored his presence, listening more attentively to one another.

5. Mentor and Guide

If others seek support, step into mentorship. Share not only successes but struggles, showing that mental freedom is a practice, not perfection. Mentorship amplifies freedom by multiplying it through others.

Passing on Freedom in Different Contexts

In Families

Children especially absorb modeled behavior. A parent who practices calm under stress teaches resilience more effectively than lectures ever could.

In Friendships

Friends often mirror one another's moods. Bringing gratitude and presence to conversations uplifts the entire dynamic.

In Workplaces

Work cultures shaped by calm, clear leaders become healthier and more productive. Passing on mental freedom at work improves both morale and output.

In Communities

Public practices—gratitude circles, meditation groups, or community service—create cultural anchors of mental clarity.

Real-World Example: The Gratitude Practice at Home

Ana and her partner began sharing one thing they appreciated about each other before bed. At first, it felt small, even awkward. But over time, it deepened their relationship, reduced conflict, and created a home culture of appreciation. By practicing gratitude together, they passed freedom into the core of their family life.

Obstacles to Passing on Mental Freedom

1. **Resistance**
   Some may dismiss practices as unnecessary or "soft." Avoid arguing; simply embody freedom. Over time, results speak louder.
2. **Over-Eagerness**
   Trying to force change often backfires. Passing freedom is about gentle influence, not pressure.
3. **Hypocrisy Risk**
   Sharing practices without living them undermines credibility. Authenticity is essential.

The Neuroscience of Shared Freedom

Neuroscience shows that human brains sync in interaction—a phenomenon called **interpersonal neural synchrony.** Calm breathing, eye contact, and presence can literally regulate others' nervous systems. This means that living with freedom helps others feel freer on a biological level.

The Deeper Lesson: Freedom Multiplies When Shared

Takeaway: Be the Anchor for Others

Passing on mental freedom is not about being a guru—it is about being an anchor. By embodying clarity, gratitude, and presence, you offer stability in a chaotic world.

The ultimate test of mental freedom is not whether you can find peace alone, but whether you can carry it into relationships, communities, and the world. When you live as an anchor of freedom, you give others permission to free their minds too.

Glossary

Accountability Partner – A trusted person who supports and checks in on your progress, helping you maintain consistency with your growth practices.

Affirmations – Positive statements repeated to reinforce a belief. Most effective when paired with evidence and action, rather than empty repetition.

Amygdala – The brain's "alarm system" that triggers fear and stress responses; mindfulness and breathwork help regulate its activity.

Anchoring Rituals – Simple, repeatable practices (such as journaling or meditation) that ground you in clarity and presence.

Autopilot Thinking – Unconscious, habitual thought patterns that drive behavior without awareness, often leading to limiting beliefs.

Boundaries – Healthy limits set in relationships, work, and digital life to protect clarity, energy, and emotional well-being.

Box Breathing – A breathwork technique involving inhaling, holding, exhaling, and holding again for equal counts (commonly 4-4-4-4). Used for stress regulation.

Cognitive Dissonance – The discomfort felt when behavior and beliefs don't align, often triggered by affirmations that feel untrue.

Cognitive Reframing – The practice of intentionally shifting perspective on a situation to see it in a more constructive or empowering way.

Community Anchors – Relationships and groups that stabilize and support mental freedom by reinforcing positive behaviors and attitudes.

Default Mode Network (DMN) – A brain network active during mind-wandering and rumination; calms down with mindfulness and presence practices.

Decision Fatigue – Mental exhaustion from making too many decisions, reducing clarity and willpower. Prevented by routines and simplifying choices.

Detachment – The ability to let go of unhealthy attachment to outcomes or people, without becoming indifferent or unfeeling.

Emotional Hijack – When strong emotions override rational thinking, often driven by amygdala activation.

Emotional Intelligence (EQ) – The ability to understand, regulate, and manage your own emotions while empathizing with others.

Evidence-Based Affirmations – Affirmations grounded in real or achievable actions, such as "I am learning to stay calm under pressure."

Flow State – A mental state of deep focus where challenge and skill are balanced, creating high performance and effortless immersion.

Future Self-Journaling – Writing from the perspective of your future self to clarify vision, align daily actions, and strengthen identity.

Gratitude Journal – A daily practice of writing down specific things you are grateful for, proven to increase happiness and resilience.

Growth Identity – Seeing yourself as an evolving person capable of learning and change, rather than fixed in one unchangeable identity.

Identity Loop – The cycle where beliefs shape actions, actions provide evidence, and evidence reinforces beliefs.

Keystone Habits – Foundational habits (like exercise, journaling, or sleep) that trigger positive ripple effects across other areas of life.

Limiting Beliefs – Deeply held negative assumptions about oneself or the world that restrict growth and freedom.

Mental Clarity – A state of calm, focused awareness where thought is not clouded by stress, distraction, or overthinking.

Mental Freedom – The ability to choose thoughts, beliefs, and reactions intentionally, free from automatic mental traps.

Micro-Actions – Small, simple steps that create consistent evidence of a new identity or habit.

Mind-Body Connection – The scientific understanding that mental and emotional states directly affect physical health, and vice versa.

Mindfulness – Paying deliberate, nonjudgmental attention to the present moment, noticing thoughts and feelings without attachment.

Multitasking Myth – The false belief that doing many things at once increases productivity. In reality, it fragments attention and lowers clarity.

Neuroplasticity – The brain's ability to rewire itself by forming new neural pathways through repeated thought and action.

Overthinking Loop – The repetitive cycle of worry, analysis, and doubt that prevents clarity and action.

Parasympathetic Nervous System (PNS) – The "rest and digest" system that calms the body and mind, often activated through slow breathing.

Presence – The practice of being fully engaged in the current moment, rather than lost in past regrets or future worries.

Reframing – A mental skill of interpreting situations in more empowering ways (e.g., rejection as redirection).

Resilience – The capacity to recover and grow from setbacks, built through reframing, community, and consistent practices.

Scarcity Mindset – Believing resources, opportunities, or love are limited, which creates fear and comparison. Opposite of abundance mindset.

Self-Compassion – Treating yourself with the same kindness you would offer a friend, essential for rewriting limiting stories.

Self-Image – The mental picture of who you believe you are; shaped by past experiences and rewritten through small wins.

Sensory Grounding – A presence practice where you anchor awareness through the five senses to calm overthinking.

Stillness – Intentional pauses of quiet and reflection that restore clarity, creativity, and emotional balance.

Stress Response – The physiological reaction triggered by perceived threats; regulated through breathwork, mindfulness, and perspective.

Triggers – Stimuli that activate strong emotional reactions, often linked to past experiences or unresolved beliefs.

Visualization – Using mental imagery to rehearse desired outcomes or create calming mental states, strengthening both performance and peace.

Victim Story – A limiting narrative where life is seen as happening *to you* rather than *through you* or *for you.*

Voting for Identity – Each small action serves as a "vote" for the person you are becoming, gradually shifting self-image.

Weekly Reflection – A structured review of wins, challenges, and adjustments that keeps clarity intentional and sustainable.

Thank You for Reading

I hope this book has given you practical tools, fresh insights, and the clarity to begin living with greater freedom of mind. Writing it was a journey of reflection and growth, and I am grateful you chose to spend your time with these pages.

If this book has helped you in any way, the most powerful way you can support it—and help others discover it—is by leaving a review on Amazon. Even a few sentences about what you found valuable makes a tremendous difference.

Your words not only encourage me as an author but also guide future readers who are searching for the same freedom and clarity you've begun to cultivate.

Thank you again for being part of this journey. May your mind remain free, focused, and open to growth.

-Eric LeBouthillier

www.ingramcontent.com/pod-product-compliance
Lightning Source LLC
Chambersburg PA
CBHW071712120626
46550CB00001B/204